POETRY AND OTHER NONSENSE

A COLLECTION OF VERSES

By

GUS BARRETT
QUALICUM BEACH, B.C.

Note for Librarians: A cataloguing record for this book is available from Library and Archives
Canada at www.collectionscanada.ca/amicus/index-e.html
ISBN 1-4120-6162-8

*Printed in Victoria, BC, Canada. Printed on paper with minimum 30% recycled fibre. Trafford's print shop
runs on "green energy" from solar, wind and other environmentally-friendly power sources.*

TRAFFORD
PUBLISHING™

Offices in Canada, USA, Ireland and UK
This book was published *on-demand* in cooperation with Trafford Publishing. On-demand
publishing is a unique process and service of making a book available for retail sale to the
public taking advantage of on-demand manufacturing and Internet marketing. On-demand
publishing includes promotions, retail sales, manufacturing, order fulfilment, accounting and
collecting royalties on behalf of the author.

Book sales for North America and international:
Trafford Publishing, 6E–2333 Government St.,
Victoria, BC v8t 4p4 CANADA
phone 250 383 6864 (toll-free 1 888 232 4444)
fax 250 383 6804; email to orders@trafford.com
Book sales in Europe:
Trafford Publishing (uk) Ltd., Enterprise House, Wistaston Road Business Centre,
Wistaston Road, Crewe, Cheshire cw2 7rp UNITED KINGDOM
phone 01270 251 396 (local rate 0845 230 9601)
facsimile 01270 254 983; orders.uk@trafford.com
Order online at:
trafford.com/05-1063

10 9 8 7 6 5 4 3 2 1

ACCOLADES

For my wife, Blanche, who shared many of the memories and created many more. For her editing, her encouragement and her patience while I was spending so much time at the computer.

For our offspring Janice, Sharon and Bill for being the wonderful people they are, and for grandkids, Kelly, Andrew, Nick, Alex and Syd, who make it all worthwhile. Thanks also to all the many friends who have encouraged me to write and kept nagging me to have it published. Now if they'll just buy a book....

INDEX

INTRODUCTION

The verses found within this book are mine,
The content is dependent on my mood.
Some, you'll find are of the trivia kind,
But I've been told that some of them are good.

They're written, not for fortune or for fame,
Financial gain is surely not the measure.
If you find I'm not expert at the game,
I'm not concerned; I do it just for pleasure.

So, if you like, read on, just take your time.
I hope you'll find something that you like.
If so, I stand, contented with my rhymes.
If not, just close the book and take a hike.

KELLY LEE

When you were just a little girl,
Maybe two or three,
You'd often come to Qualicum
To visit nana and me.
You loved to walk the sandy beach
Collecting pretty shells,
And often, clinging to our hands,
Go wading through the swells.

Then when you finally tired out
You'd always come to me,
And with your special blanket
You would climb upon my knee.
You'd give me hugs and kisses,
And beguile me with your charms,
And then without a whimper
You'd fall asleep in papa's arms.

Now you're a young lady,
All grown up and fancy free.
A busy life with little time
To visit nan and me.
But that is as it should be,
And I love you just as well,
Because, to me, you'll always be
My little "Super Kell".

BISHOPS COVE

A stretch of gravel road, a mile or two perhaps,
A fishing village perched beside the sea.
So small, it can't be found on many maps
But memories keep coming back to me.
Of growing up, the places where we played,
Of trouting poles, of rolling hoops, and tops.
Of randying on slides our fathers made,
Down snow clad hills, the fun that never stops.

Of Uncle Joe's stage head, of sculpins caught,
Of Bella's Plain, the boats we sailed, the brook.
Of Bonfire Night, the barrels that we burned.
(And also of the barrels that we took.)
Of berry picking out upon the hills,
A stop for lunch of "lassy bread" and tea.
A dip in Neddy Smith's pond, so cold it chills.
How it all keeps coming back to me.

The house upon the hill, where once I dwelt,
Looks out across the bay at Mad Rock Cove.
The rollers breaking on the rocks, I felt,
Were calling me to leave it all and rove.
And as I grew older I well knew,
That I would go away forever more.
But I never will forget the friends I knew
Where I grew up, along that rocky shore.

Where are they now, the boys and girls I knew?
"You never can go home again", 'tis said.
My bosom buddy sailed in navy blue,
While I went north to wear the coat of red.
Some stayed and built a life and prospered there,
Some live in towns and cities, countrywide.
Some have troubles that are difficult to bear,
And sometimes I hear that, sadly, one has died.

But, sometimes I wonder if, like me, they harken back
To a time when we were young and full of schemes.

3

When we didn't have much money, but there never was a lack
Of fun and joy and happiness, and dreams.
Do they see that rocky coastline; see the meadows and the banks,
See the flocks of seagulls soaring up above?
And do they sometimes bow their heads and offer up their thanks,
For the lessons that we learned, in Bishops Cove.

DAWSON CITY

There's a place up north in the Yukon
That my loving wife calls home,
Situated on the river bank
Below the midnight dome.
Where the endless summer sunshine
Makes the blossoms oh, so pretty,
It's a friendly little hamlet,
That we know as Dawson City.

Its founders were a hardy breed
Of rugged pioneers,
Men and women from 'round the world
Who pushed aside their fears.
And took the trail of ninety eight,
In that famous Klondike rush,
And, with blood and sweat and sacrifice,
Carved a city from the bush.

They landed on the muddy flat,
Beneath that gaping slide.
And with broad axes and bucksaws,
Went into the countryside.
They cut the logs and hauled them
To that flat beside the stream.
They built their town, and in doing so
They built themselves a dream.

Throughout the years they searched for gold,
Toiling in the frozen muck.
Some struck it rich, while others failed,
Much depending on ones luck.
As time went by, gold petered out,
No mother lode was found.
Some moved on, but when they did
They left behind, a town.

Dawson City's been there now
For a hundred years and more.
Still situated 'neath the dome,

5

On the Yukon River shore.
What of those hardy pioneers,
And their dream so everlasting?
The graves up on the hillside
Tell the story of their passing.

GOODBYE OLD FRIEND

Goodbye old friend,
I'm sad to see you go,
We'll never walk
Those hunting trails again.
I'll walk alone
The next time that I go,
Yet I'm grateful for the
Ending of your pain.

We've trod the trails
Where once stampeders trod,
In that vast land where
Snowcapped mountains soar.
Trails that brought us
Nearer to our God,
And memories to
Treasure evermore.

A friendship such as
Some men only dream,
'Nigh fifty years
And not one angry voice.
We'll meet again on
The far side of the stream,
Goodbye old friend,
Our God has made his choice.

HOME

My house holds all my special things
Like books and favorite chair,
And yet it only seems like home,
Whenever you are there.
The cozy house and garden,
Bring me pleasure, it is true,
But still and all, it's only home
If I am there with you.

When I come in and you're not there,
Clouds follow me inside.
Each room is dark and gloomy,
With no pleasant place to hide.
Then I hear your footsteps,
And I know you're home again.
Each time you open up the door,
You bring the sunshine in.

I could be in a crowd and yet,
Be lonely all the while,
Until I see you across the room,
And you look at me and smile.
Then I know it makes no difference,
Just where on earth I roam.
One thing is ever constant,
If you are there, I'm home.

MEMORIES OF LONG AGO

Rocky coastline rising from the sea,
Rollers breaking in upon the strand.
Fishing village perched precariously
My memory of home, my Newfoundland.

Fishing stages in every nook and cove,
The smells of salt, of steam-tarred line and sweat,
Brawny seamen performing chores they love,
Preparing to set sail to tend their nets.

Blinding hail and sleet and driving rain,
Raging storms that lash the rocky shore.
Women peeking through the windowpane.
To see a sail, and know he's back once more.

Children trudging glumly off to school,
Toting splits and copybooks and slates.
To suffer through three R's and golden rule.
Then rush off to the beach, adventure waits.

Pitching buttons, rolling hoops and tops,
Bamboo poles and bobbers painted red.
Picket fences, roving sheep to stop,
Poppies blooming in the flower bed.

Jigging tom-cods, sculpins, conners, flounders,
Toutens made from freshly kneaded dough,
Evening meal of fish and brewis or rounders.
The kerosene lamp spreads its welcome glow.

Quiet Sunday mornings, calm and still,
Boats at anchor, resting in the bay.
Men and women trudging up the hill,
Off to church to sing their hymns and pray.

Picking berries, making hay and chopping wood,
Preparing for the winter storms to come.
Christmas time, the effort to be good,
Mummering, and perhaps, a taste of rum.

9

Randying and skating in the cold
Dressed in hand-me-downs and leaky boots.
Memories that I am very proud to hold,
They've made me what I am, they are my roots.

VALHALLA

The sun's shining bright as I sit on the patio
Watching the snowbirds surrounding the pool.
All of them seniors, gray haired and wrinkled,
Finished with working, they've laid down their tools.

Sitting in lawn chairs, laying on lounges,
All settled in with their backs to the sun.
Some brown as berries, some red as lobsters,
Enjoying the good life and all having fun.

Some bob in the water like corks in the ocean,
Some sit in the shallows, unable to swim.
They're wearing sunglasses for eyesight protection,
And wearing old hats with a wide Texas brim.

They're happy to be here, far from reality,
Far from the workingman's troubles and strife.
They talk about business, fishing or farming,
All of the things that they did in "real life".

For this is Valhalla, where nothing is real,
We're all sitting here with our heads in the clouds.
And sadly, one morning we'll wake and it's gone.
And we'll all be back home with the bustling crowds.

We'll all be back home with our kids and grandchildren,
Telling our stories and waiting for when,
With the first heavy frost or the first chilly rainstorm,
We'll all rush back down to Valhalla again.

LOUISE LAKE

There's a lake nestled deep in a valley
'Neath the snowcapped Yukon hills.
Where our family romped in the summer
When the valley was peaceful and still.

A rustic old cabin once stood there,
In the jack pines that grow on the shore.
Its now just a shack, but in dreams I go back,
To see that old cabin once more.

To fish in the lake in the evening,
By the light of the big yellow moon.
Then sleep the sleep of the contented,
And awake to the call of the loon.

To watch the big rainbow trout leaping,
Near the bank where the fox kittens play.
Hear the far off howl of a timber wolf
Who successfully ran down his prey.

To return to the cabin in darkness,
Where the lamp lighted windows bring joy.
See the faces that peer from the window,
A young woman, two girls and a boy.

Now the valley and lake are just memories,
Of a time we were young and alive.
As we worked through the long Yukon winter,
And waited for spring to arrive.

God must have been proud when he made them,
And looked down from His throne up above,
For He flooded that lake with contentment,
And heaped up the valley with love.

A VERY WEALTHY MAN

I've amassed a store of wealth,
All given to me freely.
Although, to see me walking by,
You wouldn't know it, really.
I do not speak of stocks and bonds,
Or money I have hid,
I've invested in hugs and kisses,
And memories of my kids.

I've memories of diapers,
Hung waving in the breeze,
Of dirty handprints on my shirt,
And water on my knees.
There are memories of Yukon days,
Of sleigh rides in the snow,
And good-by hugs and kisses
As off to school they'd go.

I've memories of softball games,
Of playing with a pup,
Times of laughter, drying tears
All part of growing up.
There are memories of swimming pools,
And Saturday matinees,
Going out to picnics
On those gorgeous summer days.

Memories of camping trips
And fishing at the lake.
Memories of Father's Day,
Of cards and gifts they'd make.
And now that they have grown and gone,
If I'm ever down or sad,
I recall those hugs and kisses, and
"Good night, I love you dad."

Oh yes, I am a wealthy man
By any measurement.
Whether I am in a castle,

13

Or I'm living in a tent.
Because, with memories like mine,
It's plain for all to see,
If he hasn't children of his own,
Bill Gates would envy me.

THE LITTLE FISHERMAN

While walking by a pond one day,
For solitude I'm wishing,
When out upon a rock, I spied
A little fellow fishing.
He had, in hand, a willow pole,
With shopping string attached,
A bobber and a baited hook,
A twig to hold his catch.

He basked in summer sunshine.
With an air that nothing mattered,
Although his suntanned feet were bare,
And jeans and shirt were tattered.
I thought of all the fancy rods,
And other special gear,
We adults waste our money on
For fishing every year.

I wonder why we need so much,
And where have we gone wrong,
When suddenly the little fellow's
Voice broke out in song.
Then picking up his string of trout
And shouldering his pole,
He's singing as he walks away
From his favorite fishing hole,

How happily he wends his way,
No reason here for sorrow.
He'll sleep the sleep of innocence,
Then fish again tomorrow.
Now the vision disappears,
It was just a memory,
'Twas over sixty years ago,
And that little boy was me.

THE OLD MAN AT THE BEACH

He sat on a bench with his bag of bread,
Feeding the ravenous gulls and crows.
Sun beating down on his snow-white head,
Enjoying each moment before he goes.
Youthful joggers pass back and forth,
They bask in the sunshine gratefully.
He smiles to himself at a secret thought,
Then waves and turns back t'wards the sea.

What does he see as he sits and stares,
I search, but nothing appears to me.
Is it a ship for which he cares,
Or maybe just something that used to be.
I walk on by, but I turn and peek,
There's something about him that draws me back
A tear rolls down his wrinkled cheek,
And he brushes it off with his paper sack.

Is he a vet who survived the war,
Recalling the days of his distant youth?
Thinking of friends who have gone before,
Dying for what they believed was truth.
Or is it a loved one that he sees,
Someone who left him and went ahead?
He savors the smell of the flowers and trees,
Then just for a moment, he bows his head.

The sack is empty; the birds have flown,
There's just he and I and the empty sea.
The joggers along the walk have gone.
He smiles again and he nods to me.
Then he turns away with his empty sack,
Going back to his home, I know not where.
Shuffling footsteps carry him back.
Will he be alone, or does someone care?

RECOVERY

I walk alone in the beauty of the early
Morning sunshine, but I do not see,
Because of the darkness within me.
Suddenly I hear a footstep,
And you are walking beside me again.
My step quickens,
And everything is beautiful.

GROWING OLD TOGETHER

I've known you almost fifty years,
And it's still beyond my ken,
How you can look the same today,
As you used to way back then.
You don't seem any older,
And I really don't know whether
It's because you have eternal youth,
Or we're growing old together.

We've passed a lot of milestones,
Since those days when first we met,
And I'm sure we'll pass some others
'Cause we're not finished yet.
We've still a lot of dreams to fill,
We're two birds of a feather.
And nothing's going to stop us now
From growing old together.

We still have many hills to climb,
And many sights to see,
The future holds no terror, just
As long as you're with me.
And when we're feeling weary,
We can stop and smell the heather,
I have no fear of aging, for
We're growing old together.

And some day, down the road a piece
When we are forced to stop and rest,
When the body and the spirit
Can no longer stand the test.
We'll stay at home and reminisce,
There's naught I'd rather do,
Than remember all the fun I've had
While growing old with you.

MY GOLF GAME

My golf course is a perfect place,
I go there to unwind.
Whenever I'm within its bounds
I leave all cares behind.

I clean my clubs and mark my ball
And put them in the car,
Then head out for the clubhouse,
Where all my buddies are.

I practice on the putting green,
I swing a club or two.
The calcium is breaking loose,
The aches and pains are few.

My foursome now is ready,
The starter calls my name.
My hand and eye are steady,
And I'm ready for the game.

I stand upon the first tee,
The scene that greets my eye
Is one of peace and beauty,
Shimmering sea and sky.

The fairway's like a carpet,
And likewise is the green,
Except for several divots
Where the previous foursome's been.

I check my stance, a practice swing,
I flex my knees and wiggle.
And somewhere in the background,
I hear my partner giggle.

Keep the head down, follow through,
If I do it right, let's face it.
A little luck, a member's bounce,
No reason I can't ace it.

My swing is pure perfection,
I stand and watch the green
Hoping my club selection
Was all it should have been.

My partner's looking angry,
And he's coming after me.
I look, and there's my @#%^& ball
Still sitting on the tee.

WISHES FOR MY GRANDDAUGHTER

Our little Alex just turned nine,
Oh, what an age for one to be.
So many years ahead of her,
So many things for her to see.
Here's how I'd wish her world to be,
When she is just as old as me.

I wish that during her life span,
All nations will unite in peace,
And put an end to battle fields,
Where men of power and greed have lease.
For if the threat of war were gone,
Oh what a victory they'd have won.

I wish that she would always have
Freedom to stand and state her case,
Sense to know what's right and wrong,
The strength to hold her rightful place.
If she has these, I would dare to say,
She'll meet all challenges on her way.

And though she may not understand,
(She's only nine years old of late.)
I wish some day she'd see the end
Of racial bigotry and hate,
See people stand, where few have stood,
And work for peace and brotherhood.

I wish for her, clean air to breathe,
Pure water and abundant food.
The love of family and friends,
Happiness, health, and all things good.
And then, when she's as old as me,
A grandchild just as sweet as she.

21

THE HUNTER

The hunter stands in the trees beyond,
Sharp eyes scanning the lily pond,
At the ready, gun slung loose,
Awaiting that elusive moose.
A willow snaps, his eyes swing back,
To witness an enormous rack
Of antlers exiting the bush.
("Easy now, no need to rush").

The mighty bull stands on the beach
And strives, the lily pads to reach,
He stands majestic, wild and free,
Quite unaware that his enemy
Is taking aim and making plans,
To drop his moose upon the sands.
He knows that this will now complete
His winter-long supply of meat.

Then from out the tangled vines,
Comes a cow moose with calf behind.
She stands beside the bull and feeds
On lily pads and grass and weeds.
The calf bleats to express his need,
(Too tiny yet, for adult feed).
Then from her udder, soft as silk,
He sates himself with mother's milk.

The hunter stares, all motion freezes,
The pressure on the trigger eases,
He thinks of his wife and little one,
Then smiles and slowly lowers his gun.
He snaps a branch on a willow tree,
And watches the moose as they turn to flee.
He may regret the loss of meat,
But rejoice in a family still complete.

BEAUTY

The gnarled and twisted cactus grows
With giant arms held high.
It's sharpened needles take a pose,
To daunt unwary passers by.

The cactus is, to man, no good.
Its value offers nothing,
Adds not a calorie to his food,
Nor firewood for cutting.

He cannot turn it into wood,
From which to build his shelter,
Nor have it used for any good,
By mill nor plant, nor smelter.

To man, its just a useless weed,
That grows on arid waste.
Producing fruit that is, indeed,
Unfit for any taste.

And yet, this prickly useless thing
Will strive with all its powers,
To produce, in early spring,
The most delicate of flowers.

And too, its thorny branches,
That are spurned and scorned by men,
Offer home and sanctuary to
The nesting cactus wren.

I guess it's something that we learn
As we keep getting older,
That beauty is, as it's always been,
In the eye of the beholder.

THE FUTURE

When I was just a little boy,
I stood beside the sea,
And wondered what the future
Would have in store for me.

The moonlight on the ocean,
As I walked along the strand,
Seemed to whisper that my future
Was not in Newfoundland.

I asked that moon to guide me
In what should be my quest.
The moon looked down and smiled at me,
Go west young laddie, west.

So when I reached my adult years,
I happily sallied forth,
But on the journey westward,
I diverted to the north.

I reached the Klondike Valley
And there beside the stream,
I found a golden nugget,
The girl of all my dreams.

Many years have passed since then,
We're settled in the west.
That same old moon shines down on me,
And figures he knew best.

He may not be so smart at that,
Though his advice I sought,
For though my future's in the west,
My heart is in the north.

ASSETS

You have listed all your assets, got them entered in a book,
You can tell your total net worth by a brief but careful look.
Yes you've totaled up your assets and you think you're doing grand,
But there's something about assets that you just don't understand.

Your money is only paper that was never meant to last,
Your dollar is in trouble and depreciating fast.
Your stocks and bonds and RSPs that you're counting on for cash,
Could be wiped out in a moment with another market crash.

The home up in the city and the cabin at the lake,
Are mortgaged to the hilt for the investments that you make.
Your cars and other playthings are just tin and plastic trash,
And instead of being assets are a burden on your cash.

Work it out and you will find you're not so rich at all,
All those worldly goods you have are set up for a fall.
So go ahead and total up, you'll find that in the end
The only thing you've got that's worth a tinker's dam is friends.

S.S. KLONDIKE

She sits on the riverbank, old and worn,
High above the raging stream.
Her paddle wheel will turn no more,
No caulking in her seams.
The tourists on her crowded deck,
Hear stories of her former glory.
But can they really understand,
The steamship "Klondike's" story.

If she could talk, she'd tell them tales
To fill their minds with wonder,
Of men and women she has brought
To the gold fields, way off yonder.
On the final leg of that long, long trail,
That leads on to Dawson Town.
In the heart of the famous Klondike,
The valley where gold was found.

She'd tell them of fervent hopes and dreams
Of the men in search of gold,
As they sat at night in her dining lounge,
Watching the river unfold.
She'd tell of the gamblers, the hangers on,
Who always followed the throng,
To pick the pockets of honest men
While they plied them with booze and song.

She could tell of romance, of young couples who danced
In her lounge as the nights wore on.
And the physical wrecks who slept on her decks,
Returning with fortunes gone.
The good and the bad, she's carried them all,
The successful and those who failed,
And many who suffered hardships untold,
But to die at the end of the trail.

So if you're on board with the tourist horde,
Close your eyes and flow with the river.
And you may hear the squeal of her paddle wheel,

Or feel her timbers quiver.
As she strives once more to leave the shore,
And steam on to Dawson Town.
And she'll take you there, to the shimmering creeks,
Where the golden nuggets abound.

SUNSET AT QUALICUM

As shadows lengthen on the sandy beach,
Feeding sea birds flee to sheltered nests,
Eagles standing watch upon their perch,
Retreat into the forest, time for rest.

Strollers stop to breathe the evening air,
Shading their eyes from sun that lingers yet.
Watching the waves that gently lap the shore,
Then walk away, in rosy silhouette.

And on the golf links, high above the beach,
Players strive to finish one more hole.
Then stand upon that green within their reach,
And marvel at the scene that they behold.

The setting sun turns blue-green ocean waves
To brilliant shades of pink and red and gold.
The village clock chimes out the passing time,
While evening breezes go from warm to cold.

Now, as the sun blends slowly with the sea,
The brilliant colours fade, the light is gone.
And strollers turn for home as, silently,
Darkness comes, another day is done.

GETTING OLD

I've got eyeglasses for driving,
I've got a pair for sun.
And if I want to read a book,
I've yet another one.
I recently bought hearing aids,
For me, a new adventure,
Then, just to top it off, I bought
A brand new set of dentures.

Then, after buying eyeglasses,
My hearing aids, and teeth,
I found that, next, I needed
Some orthotics for my feet.
I take pills for my arthritis,
And some for ulcers too.
Vitamins to build me up,
And to ward off Asian flu.

What little hair I have is gray,
What I had on top, I've shed,
I'm getting stooped and slowing down,
Long past my prime in bed.
Still, looking on the brighter side,
I thank my lucky stars,
Each morning when the sun comes up
And I'm still above the grass.

THE DENTIST'S CHAIR

We all have things that bug us,
Things that make us sore,
The things that I enjoy the most,
Might irk you to the core.
I will not eat cottage cheese,
While others lap it up,
Yet they are quite disgusted,
When I put sugar in my cup.

My friends love playing in the snow,
While I think winter stinks.
The only way that I like ice is,
As an additive to drinks.
I could play golf every day
From early spring through fall.
But others think its stupid,
To be talking to a ball.

There are those who like to exercise,
I'd rather sit and think.
I could be writing poetry
While you're skating at the rink.
And if you like to surf the waves
Go right ahead, get wet.
As for me, I'd rather do
My surfing on the net.

We all like things that please us,
And dislike the things that don't.
You may watch ballet or opera,
But, you can your bet your boots I won't.
Yet, on one thing we're in agreement,
One that we all hate and fear,
That is, sitting there, white knuckled,
In that # $@%& dentist's chair.

NATURE'S LAW

She perches in the "eagle tree,"
That stands beside the beach.
Sharp eyes searching, ever searching,
For food within her reach.
Movement 'neath the ocean's surface,
Is captured by that searching eye,
With majestic wings outstretched
The eagle hovers in the sky.

Circling over shallow waters,
Where the feeding salmon lies,
Unaware of looming peril
From the mistress of the skies.
Suddenly a passing shadow,
Sends them fleeing for their lives,
But too late, for high above,
The mighty eagle swoops and dives.

Fearsome talons slash the surface,
Then once more the eagle soars,
While a silver salmon struggles
In the prison of her claws.
The hunter takes the victim
To her nest of mud and sticks.
She tears the flesh from off the bone,
To feed her hungry chicks.

And so it is, the salmon dies
To feed the eagle once again.
That's the way it's meant to be,
It's just a link in nature's chain.
Have no weeping for the victim,
Do not rage against the claw,
It's survival of the fittest,
That is Mother Nature's law.

GOLFER'S LAMENT

I thought the drive was excellent,
My swing was straight and true,
The ball was humming sweetly,
As through the air it flew.
Rising slightly as it sped,
I watched the path it took,
Like an arrow t'wards the green,
And then, that awful hook.
It kept on turning to the left,
As down the course I strode,
Until I heard that solid "smack"
Oh God!!! It's on the road.

Back to the tee, I try again,
It's only a par three.
I wonder why the golf Gods
Keep on doing this to me.
This time my swing is perfect.
(Like every swing I take.)
Down the fairway, across the green,
Then "Splash", into the lake.
Dear God, you know I don't ask much,
I willingly play my role,
But, just once, to hear the others say,
"Good shot, It's in the hole."

FITNESS

These summer days I find it wise,
To get outside and exercise,
Instead of sitting round and talking,
I'm really getting into walking.

When I go out, it never fails,
I meet old-timers on the trails.
Some are jogging some are hiking,
While others go for mountain biking.

An ancient lady passed me by,
At a speed that I considered high.
She looked so vibrant, trim and neat
With those roller blades upon her feet.

Right behind her, gaining fast,
An old gent on his scooter passed,
Protective padding on his knees,
Pigtail flowing in the breeze.

She turned and flirted, openly
He grinned as he passed and winked at me.
Then down a quiet trail they went,
Like two teenagers, heaven bent.

I stared, my thoughts I dare not mention,
But I could guess at their intention,
As quickly down a hill they drove,
Then turned into a sheltered grove.

My presence I knew was not required.
I turn for home; I'm getting tired.
This fitness thing is not a snap.
I think I'll go and take a nap.

POLITICS

There was a time when I was young,
I was naïve and trusting,
Then I met a politician who
Was out upon the hustings.
He taught me all the finer points,
About deceit and guile,
Like how to screw your neighbor,
While you greet him with a smile.

He said, "It's not a crime, you know,
To lie and cheat and scheme.
The lining of his pockets,
Is any politicians dream."
"And though the opposition squawks
About the cream, I skim,
Would he be any different,
If the job had gone to him."

You see, he said, it's natural,
To skin the unprotected.
For that's the aim of anyone
Who ever got elected.
And if by chance, they find you out,
And accuse you of the wrong
Just hold your head up, grasp the flag,
And say, "I've done no wrong."

He never shirked his dirty deeds,
But carried on for ages.
To list his indiscretions would
Require many pages.
When finally caught, red handed,
He couldn't well defend it,
So he was banished from his seat,
And promoted to the Senate.

34

YUKON SUMMER

Clear blue skies above us,
Days of endless sun,
Summer is upon us,
Days of endless fun.
Heavy coats and moccasins,
Have all been packed away,
In the hope that, this time,
Summer's here to stay.

Grayling in the crystal stream,
Leaping for the fly,
Happy fishermen can dream
'Cause holidays are nigh.
Swimming in the lake for hours,
Camping in the trees,
The sweet bouquet of wild flowers
Wafting on the breeze.

Lovers strolling in the park,
Children on vacation,
People tending flower beds,
Toil and perspiration.
Smiling faces everywhere,
Happiness and bliss.
God, if we could only have
Every day like this.

DAWSON REVISITED

I stood on the dome overlooking the town,
And I could not believe what I saw.
The changes that fifty odd years have brought 'round
Astounds me, and sticks in my craw.
The faces of strangers I see all around
But seldom the face of a friend.
And I think of my days as a policeman in town,
And I wonder, is this how it ends?

There aren't any river front docks anymore,
No more paddle wheels churning the stream.
The sight of those sternwheelers lining the shore,
Is a memory, a vision, a dream.
The graveyard's still there all covered with wood.
I can still see the scar of the slide.
I can still see the island where Lousetown once stood,
In the midst of the river so wide.

Where are the old buildings that tilted and turned,
In tune with the permafrost's will?
Restored, fallen down, hauled away or burned.
But the memories are living there still.
And where has my barracks with the old canons gone,
Where I once proudly served as a lad.
Replaced by new buildings, with flowers and lawn,
It's restricted, it's secure, and it's sad.

I gaze up the valley, see the tailings still there,
All barren deserted and grim.
And I think of the days when the dredges were here,
And our cup runeth full to the brim.
When old timers lived in their shacks on the creeks,
Independent, with shovel and pan.
Each with his own private dream as he seeks
For gold where the clear waters ran.

Now there are great caterpillars and such
All ripping up acres of ground.
The creeks are all muddy, and there is very much

36

Desolation and wreckage around.
It is progress I know, and we're going to be
So much better off in the end.
Yet I gaze at the river, and I wish I could see
A sternwheeler rounding the bend.

ON BOARD THE SOURDOUGH

Out on board the Sourdough, at anchor in the bay,
Sunset to the westward marks the passing of the day.
The boat's secured for sleeping; the clean up chores are done,
We're sitting in the stern to catch those final rays of sun.
We've feasted on the finest food, a virtual repast.
And now we sit contented, with brandy in our glass.
Telling stories of adventures that we had in days of yore
And it really doesn't matter that we've heard them all before.

When the evening breezes freshen and the brandy bottle's dry,
We crawl into our sleeping bags with a deep-contented sigh.
With the gently rolling motion of the boat upon the deep,
I soon forget reality and drift away in sleep.
I sleep a deep and dreamless sleep, refreshed when I awaken.
To the wonderful aroma of Harry frying bacon.
Then when breakfast's over and we've washed the final dish,
With the motor humming smoothly, we are off to catch a fish.

Trolling through the ebbing tide just off Deep Bay light,
With Harry at the tiller we are waiting for the bite.
The rods are slowly bobbing in their holders on the rail,
And while we wait for action, Harry's telling me a tale.
The sun is shining brightly, the reflection off the sea,
Brings a gentle warmth and feeling of contentment over me.
Then the sense of peacefulness and wonder that I feel,
Is shattered in a moment by the screeching of a reel.

In a scene of pandemonium, the hook is quickly set,
With Harry handling the rod, I'm rushing for the net.
The rod is bent and twisted; the line is drawn and tight,
Harry's holding firmly as the Coho makes his fight.

The action's brief and furious, and then the fighting stops,
As the tired, gleaming salmon rises slowly to the top.
With our Coho safely landed, we can stop and maybe gloat.
Nothing's greater to a fisherman than salmon in the boat.

Now we're heading back to port, our fishing trip is through,
The Sourdough steaming proudly, with a proud and happy crew.
The weather's warm and pleasant, with not a hint of fog,
The record of our journey has been entered in the log.
We've enjoyed our little fishing trip; our appetite's been sated,
We've reminisced and laughed again, at stories we've related.
With boat secured, we head for home with pleasant thoughts of
when,
We will step on board the Sourdough and do it all again.

PRIDE

A robin sat upon the fence,
With bright red breast a'panting,
Very interested in
The garden I was planting.

He waited till he saw a worm
In the dirt that I had dug.
A tasty little snack he'd make,
Much better than a bug.

And so the robin left his perch,
And fluttered down by me.
Then, in a flash, he grabbed the worm,
And hid behind a tree.

Then, as he slowly ate his meal,
His chest swelled up with pride,
As he thought about how skillfully,
He could hunt, then hide.

So, when he'd finished eating,
He preened and dozed, then – "Splat".
The little bugger, he forgot
About the neighbor's cat.

RUDE AWAKENING

When I left my home in fifty-one,
While still a callow youth,
I joined the Royal Mounted,
To maintain the right and truth.
They sent me off to training school
To prep for my career.
Gave me that scarlet tunic
That I was proud to wear.

For six long months they trained me
And taught me many skills,
Brass polishing, saluting,
And cleaning floors, and drills.
I learned the art of self-defense
And how not to abuse it.
They taught me how to use a gun,
Then warned me not to use it.

I learned of all the brave young men
In the history of the Force,
McLeod, and Larson, Constantine,
And Samuel Steele, of course.
They told me of the backing
And support that I could seek.
While all I need commit to them
Was seven days per week.

When done, they put me on a plane,
And sent me way up north.
Where, some fifty years before
Sam Steele had sallied forth..
They dropped me off in Dawson,
Far from home and all alone,
Then left me with these parting words,
"Son, you're on your own."

FORTUNE HUNTING

My net income has quickly diminished,
Through inflation and cutbacks and such.
They say that the good times are finished,
Though I never did have very much.
I've been struggling for a long-term solution,
While my assets have hit a new low,
Then my wife just came up with the notion,
Why not give the stock market a go.

Now, I've never had faith in those stock market buys,
I've just not been a gambling man.
My friends all assured me to purchase was wise,
And that I should buy all that I can.
This was an electronics firm that was new,
'twould be featured on the big board.
It's a great opportunity, in the long view,
My future was all but secured.

It would come on the market at just seven bucks
A wonderful bargain indeed.
They say it would peak at a hundred, with luck,
"That's an estimate, not guaranteed".
So we mortgaged our souls to the devil,
And we dived in for three thousand shares.
The broker seemed to be on the level,
For he smiled as he sold me his wares.

Then, at our computer, we watched through the day,
As the stock market started to slide.
It seemed that our future was slipping away
Like a boat on the outgoing tide.
But just before closing the trend seemed to turn,
And the price of our shares soon rebounded.
Now we smiled as we thought of our kids when they learned,
Of the massive new fortune we'd founded.

Then before we retired, with a head full of dreams.
We sat and we toasted our health

And we laughed at our plans and our outrageous schemes
To dispose of our newly found wealth.
We dreamed of new mansions with fabulous views,
And, next morning, when we awoke,
We threw back the covers and turned on the news.
And we learned that our firm had gone broke.

REMEMBRANCE DAY

Old men marching side by side,
Wearing their medals with glowing pride.
And as they stop at the monument,
One of their number, old and bent,
Approaches the shrine on shuffling feet,
With tears in his eyes he lays a wreath,
To honor the ones who have gone before,
Casualties of that distant war.

A little boy in the watching crowd,
Turns to his daddy and asks aloud,
"Tell me daddy, tell me why
All those old men stand and cry?"
He doesn't know of that ancient strife
That fight for a cause, a way of life,
Doesn't know of the youths who've died,
While loved ones stayed at home and cried.

He hasn't watched as mighty planes
Suddenly roll and crash in flames,
Or seen great ships on the ocean blue
Explode and disappear from view.
He hasn't crawled through a field of mud,
Sick of the horror and stained with blood,
While all around, the canons roar,
And young men die by the countless score.

If he understood why so many died,
He would know why old men stood and cried.
Why each succeeding year they come
And proudly march to the pipe and drum,
Shoulder to shoulder, side by side,
Wearing their honors with open pride.
He hasn't studied history yet,
Tell him daddy; lest we forget.

WALK WITH ME

Come; walk with me upon the silver sand
We'll walk the beach at the breaking of the day.
While nature's silent beauty is at hand,
And the sun is rising over Parksville Bay.
We'll see above, the giant eagles soar,
An endless flight in search of daily bread,
And hear the flocks of seagulls on the shore
Squawk an endless pleading to be fed.

Come; walk with me in early morning showers,
While overhead dark storm clouds have appeared.
We'll walk 'midst swaying trees and autumn flowers.
Remembering the good times that we've shared.
We'll walk upon the beach at ebbing tide
And feel beneath our feet, the shifting sand.
Thankful that we still stand side by side.
Then we'll walk into the future, hand in hand.

SENIORS' SKATING

"What is he doing here", well you might ask,
Lounging around at the rink.
"He's too old to be turning to skating again".
But I'm not as smart as you think.

I hadn't skated in forty-five years,
And I had no intent to return.
But my friends all assured me, like riding a bike,
"You never forget once you've learned."

So I put on some skates and stepped onto the ice,
Every muscle was already sore.
My knees they were knocking so loudly and long,
That somebody answered the door.

An old lady sped by me just floating on air,
And I thought, "that looks easy enough."
Then my skates moved with a mind of their own,
And I landed flat on my duff.

My friends gathered round as I lay on the ice,
All wondering if I had died.
I saw stars in my eyes and my face was quite red,
But the only thing hurt was my pride.

I brushed myself off and got back on my feet.
And then, just as quick as a wink.
My feet started moving in time with the tune,
And I made a full turn of the rink.

I returned to my home quite elated indeed,
With muscles so sore that I cried.
But now I can't wait to return to the ice,
For I'm really quite glad that I tried.

46

END OF AN ERA

For years they sat upon the weighs,
Planks bleaching in the sun,
A reminder to all of their glory days
On the Whitehorse to Dawson run.
On the golden trail of ninety eight,
And the great Klondike stampede,
When they carried mail and carried freight,
And men of a stronger breed.

They sat and they rotted, through the years,
As they watched the northland grow,
While sap from their timbers dripped like tears
Into the river below.
The people demanded much faster trips
To further their business deals,
And gave no thought to the crumbling ships,
With their sun warped paddlewheels.

'Till at last, came a group of vandals,
Who, in a careless act of shame,
Lit up that fatal candle
And set those famous boats in flames.
The citizens then set up a shout
As they realized the cost.
But too late to put the fire out,
A great piece of the past was lost.

FIRST LOVE

Way back when I was in grade eight,
I still thought girls were second rate
Until I met a girl of twelve,
As cute as one of Santa's elves.
An attitude so bright and sunny,
Lips so soft and sweet as honey.
'Twas puppy love I will agree
But I fell for her and she for me.

My grades declined, although I tried,
My mind was elsewhere occupied.
With daydreams of a pretty face,
My schoolwork now took second place.
I packed her books and walked her home,
I even wrote for her, a poem,
And while it did get her attention,
It caused me after school, detention.

We were not into heavy dating,
Some movie shows, or winter skating.
Of many walks we two could boast,
We made a pair for wiener roasts.
And so it went, grade nine and ten,
Until there came a moment when
We realized that in the end,
We were not lovers, only friends.

Yet, though no lasting pact ensued,
It was a pleasant interlude.
If we met today I hope I'd find,
Her life has been as good as mine.
For later, though it wasn't she,
I found the girl that was for me.
Why do these thoughts occur today?
'Twas so long ago and far away.

LOOKING BACK

There have been times, I wished I could,
Withdraw myself from fatherhood.
Times when I awoke on Christmas morn,
Dulled from sampling the corn,
To find the clock reads only three,
And yet the kids are calling me
To heed, and from my slumber pause,
To view their gifts from Santa Claus.

I leave my warm and comfy bed,
There are fairy stories to be read.
There are dolls to dress and drums to play,
"Hurry daddy, it's Christmas Day".
There are toys and games, and sleighs and skis,
And other gifts beneath the tree.
All to be opened, shown and tried.
Clothes to model bikes to ride.

By dawn the gifts have all been shown,
The house is like a battle zone.
Paper wrapping everywhere,
Juice stains on my favorite chair,
Injured dolls and broken toys.
If I could just escape the noise
And quietly go back to bed
To ease the aching in my head.

Today I wake on Christmas morn,
The house is still, the kids have gone.
Now there's only nan and me,
Alone beside the Christmas tree.
The house is quiet, trim and neat,
No pattering of little feet.
And yet, there's something that we lack,
God, if we could just go back.

THE POET AND THE ARTIST

An artist and a poet stood
Outside the Pearly Gates.
Saint Peter had decreed for now,
The two would have to wait.
Until the honour he could grant
To one, and one alone,
To occupy the single seat
Remaining near the Throne.

It should be me the painter said
Because I paint so grand,
My scenic re-creations are
In constant high demand.
With oils and brush and steady hand
I will produce a scene,
To bring a smile to the face of man
Where only gloom had been.

The poet hung his head and wept
As this testament he heard,
For all he had to offer was,
A skillful way with words.
His poems were amusing, but
They would not even start
To counteract the value of
The other fellow's art.

Saint Peter told the artist,
I too have seen first hand
The scenes that you've created
With your brush and steady hand.
But though they are skillfully done,
They're never real I fear,
They are but reproductions, for
The scene's already there.

The poet, on the other hand,
With no model at his hand,
May dream about a topic,

And, upon it will expand.
Then, using only intellect
And words that he will find,
Will etch a vivid picture
Within the human mind.

And so, a ruling has been made
On who should come inside.
A decision, irreversible,
Was broadcast heaven wide.
That, though we are indeed impressed,
With a brilliant artist's feat,
Because he has a way with words,
The poet wins the seat.

BILL

When he was just a little lad
I taught him how to fish.
And took him out on camping trips,
Which was his fondest wish.
I taught him how to cast the line,
And how to set the hook,
Which stream was good for fishing,
The likeliest place to look.

Then I taught him how to shoot,
And safely handle guns.
Shared safety and survival tips,
As fathers do with sons.
How to set a rabbit snare,
And how to pitch a tent.
To appreciate and have respect
For his environment.

We fished throughout the Yukon,
In it's crystal lakes and streams.
And I smiled, as he developed
To fulfill a father's dreams.
Then as the weekends came and went,
We roamed those distant hills,
I watched with pride as by my side
He grew and gathered skills.

Now that he's a married man
With children of his own.
I like to share the credit for
The way that he has grown.
But thinking back to those early days,
And all the fun we've had.
I know that he was teaching me
Just how to be a dad.

MARCH

Out my window, o'er the lawn,
I spy a robin on the wing.
In a moment he is gone,
Still, it's a sign that this is spring.
The grass is white with morning frost,
That yields before the rising sun,
Another battle fought and lost,
Old man Winter's on the run.

Along the walkway to my door,
The purple heather is in bloom,
It's what we've all been waiting for,
Release at last, from winter's gloom.
The climbing rosebush sprouting leaves,
Snowdrops and crocuses appear,
As Mother Nature slowly weaves
Her pattern for another year.

YUKON SPRING

Daylight hours are lengthening,
Spring is in the air.
The inner self is strengthening,
The will to live is there.
Frozen creeks are breaking up,
Cool and crystal clear.
Birds are singing in the trees,
Summer must be near.

Icicles melting from the eaves,
Grass fighting through the snow,
Sap is running to the leaves,
And pussy willows grow.
Kids are picking crocuses
Up on crocus hill,
People gain new focuses,
Newfound dreams to fill.

Soon we'll all go fishing,
We're out of winter's rut,
No more snow to shovel,
No more wood to cut.
Then we'll hold a barbecue,
Out upon the lawn,
We'll sit and raise a glass with you,
Thank God that winter's gone.

THE BUTTERFLY

The butterfly sits on a rose,
Exhausted from its flitting.
A thing of beauty and of grace,
Even while its sitting.
It sips the nectar hungrily,
Then off again it goes,
On bright and pretty spotted wings
To find another rose.

It flutters on from bloom to bloom,
Its hunger never sated,
I watched it from my living room
And wondered as I waited,
What if I had giant wings,
Would I behave that way?
Sampling the best of things,
Then quickly fly away.

I watch it as it flits along,
Wishing I too could go.
Forget the things that have gone wrong,
The things that bug me so
But yet, its life I wouldn't want.
Because, on second thought,
While it seems a simple, pleasant life,
It's also very short.

I MUST HAVE KNOWN

When you were born, I must have known,
Through some quite strange telepathy,
That after twenty years had flown,
We'd meet and you would marry me.
Else why would I, when fully grown,
Have left my home in Newfoundland,
To search a world, to me unknown,
For what, I did not understand.

But search I did, not knowing why,
Or where I might attain my goal,
And all the while, I thought that I
Was just a wandering, restless soul.
Until I reached the frozen north,
Where northern lights patrol the sky,
There I found, that which I sought,
The one I'd mold my future by.

When on a starlit arctic night,
I strode into a Whitehorse bar,
And peering through the flickering light,
I spied a table, and there you are.
Country music filled the air,
A song of broken dreams, and gloom,
But at that moment, I didn't care,
For me, your smile lit up the room.

Somehow I knew my search was done,
From some strange loneliness I'm free,
Somehow I knew you were the one,
The only one on earth for me.
Now fully fifty years have gone,
And from the North we two have flown,
But still I think, when you were born,
Somehow, deep down, I must have known.

THE GOLFERS PRAYER

Dear lord, when I depart this life,
And enter heaven's gate,
I hope they'll have a golf course there,
With reasonable rates.
With fairways that are carpet like,
All soft and green and cheery,
Greens that run true to the hole,
And gullies somewhat scary.

I hope there'll be some cherry trees
That bloom so bright each spring,
Great cedars, firs and chestnuts,
Fruit trees and everything.
If you could have some little fawns
That gambol on the green.
While mama watches proudly,
Oh Lord, that would be keen.

If fairways stretched along the beach
Of some blue rippled sea,
Where I could see the mountains
As I stand upon the tee.
And if I gaze into the sky,
And see great eagles soar,
Dear Lord, could mortals such as I,
Dare ask for any more.

If it could have great flocks of geese,
And sea lions in the spring,
Raucous crows and sea gulls,
And pretty birds that sing.
If I could stand upon the tee,
And looking far and wide,
See nothing but the beauty,
Of a peaceful countryside.

These things, dear Lord, I humbly ask,
When I go through the Gates.

As well as camaraderie
With all my golfing mates.
Then Lord I had a second thought,
For now I need not come,
'Cause all those things await me,
On the links at Qualicum.

FASCINATION

While sitting on my balcony,
More often than I oughta,
I see the fascination that
Most people have with water.
It seems they can't resist the urge
To stop and watch the breakers surge.

Seniors on their morning walk,
Will stop and, hand in hand,
Listen to the ripple of
The sea upon the sand.
Then stretch an aching frame to reach,
A pretty pebble on the beach.

Young families on a summer day,
Will sit and watch with pride
As little children romp and play
While wading in the tide.
Young voices ring like silver bells,
On sighting extra special shells.

Young couples sit in fading light,
Oblivious to weather,
And on a bench, in fond embrace,
Will plan their lives together.
Then as the sun sets on the shore,
They pledge their love forever more.

These things I know to be the truth,
It didn't just occur to me,
From grandparents to callow youth,
There's fascination with the sea.
How do I know all this, you say?
I sit and watch it every day.

REMINISCING

I sit and watch the ocean waves
Lap gently at the shore,
And as I watch, my thoughts go back
To Bishops Cove once more.
My recollections are so clear,
Yet I've been gone for fifty years.

I see the house upon a hill
Where sometimes, as a child,
I'd watch in fascination
As Atlantic storms ran wild.
And wonder how my life would be,
If I could go beyond that sea.

I see the outline of the snow
Piled high against the window pane,
As 'round the glowing stove we'd sit
To watch the raging blizzard wane.
And yet the blizzard's praise we'd sing,
It brought us snow for randying.

I see the little one room school,
Where I spent many endless days,
And learned my lessons while I longed
To spend my time in other ways.
I yearned to leave that schoolhouse door
To fish and dream along the shore.

I see that narrow gravel road
That winds its way beside the sea,
Where lovers walk and children play
In peaceful, calm serenity.
How many trysts have been bestowed,
Along that winding gravel road.

I see the little fishing boats
Set out at dawn, by twos and threes,
Skimming the waves as tiny sails,
Catch the early morning breeze.

On shore we await that moment when,
We see their safe return again.

Now I sit here, quite content,
Living once more near the sea,
Though far across the continent
From where, back then, I used to be.
But still, as through this land I rove,
My thoughts go back to Bishops Cove.

NOBAWDY HOME

A Mountie went to Dawson town,
In service to mankind,
Downhearted when he thought about
The girl he'd left behind.
He knew that while he stayed up here,
In this god-forsaken place,
He'd never find another with
Her beauty, poise and grace.

That very night, 'round midnight,
On his first all night patrol,
He chanced to meet a damsel,
At a local watering hole.
She'd a face reserved for angels,
And a form so neat and trim,
He knew in that first moment
That this jewel was meant for him.

"Hello, My name is John", he said.
"I'm here to serve mankind."
"I'd like you with me to replace,
The girl I left behind."
"Thank you, kind sir," the lass replied,
"I'll join you when I can,
You see, like you, I came up north,
To serve the needs of man".

"We each serve in our way", he said
"I'd guess you'd be a nurse,
Or kindergarten teacher teaching
Little children verse."
"I don't teach little girls," she laughed,
Just fathers and their sons,
And though I've never met you sir,
I have known a lot of Johns."

"So, while to all the Mounted Police,
My bonny hat I'll tip.
I can not accept your offer of

A long relationship.
But if, in time, the hardships of
Your service gets you down,
Come on up and see me,
I'm the Madam of this town."

MISSING YEARS

Where did that young couple go my love?
Why did they leave so soon?
Wasn't it only a week ago
That under an arctic moon,
They pledged their love to each other,
Swore to be true to the last.
How could it be, unbeknownst to me,
That half a century passed.

Where have the children gone my love?
Where have the children gone?
Wasn't it only yesterday
That the littlest one was born.
Surely they couldn't have grown so fast
They must be around somewhere.
Now that we've lots of time on our hands,
Why aren't the little ones here?

Have you noticed the years go by my love,
Have you noticed how we've aged?
Wasn't it just in the spring of the year,
The night we became engaged.
We were so young a while ago,
Maybe a month or so.
Now suddenly we are seniors,
Where did the middle age go?

THE BALLAD OF CHICKADEE

Strange tales are told in the arctic cold,
But the strangest told to me,
Was that of a hale Cape Breton male
Who was known as Chickadee.
He came north to mine in thirty-nine,
To search for gold I think,
But the search he swore, for the yellow ore
Would drive a man to drink.

He was small of frame, and he gained his name
From the squeaky voice he had.
When sober, as mild as a little child
Like a gentle Sir Galahad.
Tears would race down his grizzled face,
If a tale of woe was told.
He'd donate his time and his final dime,
To a stranger who's hungry or cold.

But give him a drink and one would think
That a tiger had broken loose,
He would sit on a stool like a drunken fool,
Till his brain was dulled by juice.
Then he'd turn about and he'd rant and shout
With scarcely the strength of a louse,
As he left the place he would punch the face
Of the biggest man in the house.

Then broken and beat, alone in the street,
He would lay in a booze-fogged peace,
Until without fail, he would land in jail,
Cared for by the mounted police.
He would get ten days for his wayward ways,
Or more if his wounds were bad.
For that iron cell that he knew so well,
Was the only "home" that he had.

One stormy night in the pale moon light,
He stumbled through the snow.
In anger chased, from his drinking place,

65

And with nowhere else to go.
In a haze he sank in a deep snow bank,
He felt warm and he thought he'd doze.
They found him at five more dead than alive,
And both his hands were froze.

He awoke that night in the glaring light,
With nurses surrounding him.
And his gaze it sped to the clean white bed,
And he noticed his missing limbs.
He remembered the fight in that arctic night,
And he thought of that awful storm.
Then he started to speak in that awful squeak,
"Thank God, my hands are warm."

THE END OF INNOCENCE

We watched in stunned silence,
On that morning in September.
A day of such destruction,
That the world will long remember.
We saw the vivid pictures,
And we heard the panicked screams,
As that thunderous explosion
Marked the end of many dreams.

We watched the wild inferno,
As the bricks and rubble fell,
And prayed as rescue workers
Walked into that flaming hell.
Then the final tragic moment
A world of smoke and sound.
When those two gigantic towers
Came cascading to the ground.

We watched as smoke and ashes
Formed into an inky shroud,
And we saw the fear and horror
On the faces in the crowd.
Then as we watched policemen strive
To reestablish order.
Our thoughts were with our many friends
Who live across the border.

We've always felt apart from strife,
Protected and secure,
But that feeling of security
Is dashed forever more.
The age of peace and innocence,
That marked this land of ours,
Was ended in that moment
When the airplanes hit the towers.

WALKING THE SEA WALL

I love to walk the sea wall
In the early morning mist.
Or in sunshine, at the dawning of the day.
To set a brisk athletic pace,
Or dawdle if I wish,
And watch the sea lions frolic in the bay.

I love to walk the sea wall
When the rain is pouring down.
When the sea gulls seek for shelter on the land,
To watch the ducks and buffle heads,
And listen to the sound
Of the gentle waves that ripple on the sand.

I love to walk the sea wall
When it's blowing up a gale,
I can look above and watch the eagles soar,
Or gaze into the distance,
See a tiny silver sail,
Or just listen to the breakers hit the shore.

I love to walk the sea wall
When the herring boats are in.
Or when salmon seek the river mouth to spawn,
When the water roils with battle
Of the flipper and the fin,
As the seal will gorge himself and then he's gone.

I love to walk the sea wall
It's a favorite haunt of mine,
There is always something changing in the sea.
No matter what the weather,
If it's me you seek to find,
Walk the sea wall, that is likely where I'll be.

REINCARNATION

Looking out across the sea
And thinking of creation.
I wonder if there really is
A true reincarnation.
If so, and if I had my wish,
I think I'd come back as a fish.

It would be fun to swim all day
In waters dark and deep,
Then hide inside a comfy bed
Of weeds, and go to sleep.
I'll be a fish by hook or crook,
If you will come back as a hook.

Then again, a great sea lion,
Is what I think I'd rather be,
So big and strong and handsome,
That you couldn't help but fall for me.
But that would only work I guess,
If you're a pretty sea-lioness.

Or I could be an octopus,
If I could be so bold to.
I'd love to have that many arms
To cuddle and enfold you.
What fun we'd have, just you and I,
Creating little octopi.

I think I'll give it some more thought,
Who knows what tribulations,
That I could bring upon myself,
With this reincarnation.
I would accept, but only when,
I'm sure you're coming back again.

69

PARENTAL GUIDANCE

This morning ere the sun came up,
A sea lion calling to her pup,
Woke me from my pleasant dreams,
Deliberately, or so it seems.

She sounded sad and so depressed,
That I got up, and scarcely dressed,
I stepped out on my patio
To see why she was crying so.

I saw her lying on a log,
Gazing out into the fog,
Searching, searching everywhere,
But still the pup did not appear.

Then from 'neath her resting place
Appeared a little impish face.
Her anguish turned to glee and then,
Her off spring laughed and dived again.

The mother dived into the sea,
Quite incensed it seemed to me,
And when she caught the little nipper
She spanked it soundly with a flipper.

A message to all parents, brave,
When your wee ones misbehave,
Though you're inclined to be a hugger,
Lay it on the little bugger.

GRANDPA'S PIPE

Grandpa smoked a briar pipe
That curled below his chin.
It seems to me he smoked it all his life.
He filled the bowl with "Beaver plug",
Then gently tamped it in,
With a calloused thumb and rusty pocketknife.

He'd light it with an ember,
That he rescued from the grate.
Then through a cloud of aromatic smoke,
He'd sit back and smile at grandma,
For many years his mate,
And he didn't seem to mind that he was broke.

He was happy with his lot in life,
Contented and secure,
Though he never had a lot that I could see.
As long as he had grandma,
He would never ask for more,
Except his pipe and grandkids at his knee.

He would puff his pipe and tell us tales,
Of fishing on the Banks.
Tales of wooden ships and iron men.
Then gazing fondly out to sea,
He would give his silent thanks,
Then smile at us and fill his pipe again.

Through the years I'd most forgotten,
Dear old grandpa and his pipe,
And the stories that he used to tell us kids.
Then he died at ninety-two,
An age considered ripe,
Still smoking "Beaver" like he always did.

POLITICALLY CORRECT

While sitting at the waterfront,
With no place else to go,
I heard the strangest argument,
'Tween a raven and a crow.
It seems it started friendly like,
As to which should be the bigger,
But escalated when the raven
Called the crow a nigger.

A passing duck could not resist
The urge to add his quack,
And offered his opinion that
The proper term was "black".
A wise old goose that overheard,
Said, as far as he could see,
The prudent phrase to use would be,
A "visible minority".

Two seagulls squawking noisily,
Said "African" was right,
But the raven wouldn't listen
Because gulls are mostly white.
While all the birds were bickering,
Creating quite a din,
It seemed to me that all of them
Were imitating men.

An eagle soaring overhead,
All bird life to protect.
Suggested that, politically,
"Coloured" would be correct.
While combatants bickered noisily,
As to which term would fit.
The eagle tired of the game
And bombed them all with shit.

BONFIRE NIGHT

It's bonfire night, November 5th.
We meet on Bella's Plain,
To celebrate by fire light,
Guy Fawkes' night once again.
We've gathered fuel for months ahead
Preparing for this night,
Some obtained by legal means,
But more by dark of night.

There are boxes from aunt Liza's store
Some trees from Papa's grove,
And splits that mom was saving
To light up the morning stove.
Freeman brought a puncheon
That was his own, he said,
But we know that it was stolen
Down at uncle Joe's stage-head.

My brothers all are there with me
Nathan, Ed and John,
We've pilfered anything flammable
That we have chanced upon.
An autumn night in Newfoundland,
The wind is cold and biting,
We sit and wait for 8 o'clock,
The hour set for lighting.

Henley arrived of course,
With little brother Max,
Each with one of uncle Bert's
Fish barrels on his back.
We laughed at Ike and Eric,
As up the hill they strove,
To push an ancient out house
Stolen way down in the cove.

Then all evening as the firelight
Reflected off the bay,
We sat and sipped dogberry wine,

73

We'd made and stashed away.
Then as the hours ticked away,
Oh, what a time we had,
We laughed and puffed on Markie's smokes,
He'd stolen from his dad.

Then a sudden clamor,
Brought me from my reverie.
I haven't been on Bella's Plain
Since nineteen forty-three.
It was oh so many years ago,
Those fires we did light,
But I remember all those boys,
And especially bonfire night.

THE HERO

They gathered at the landing field,
To bring their hero back.
Short weeks ago, he'd volunteered
For fighting in Iraq.
They cheered him then, this teenaged boy,
While wishing him God speed,
Then he went bravely to the front,
That a nation may be freed.

Now they stand in silence,
As the boy comes home once more,
Borne on the sturdy shoulders
Of his comrades in the Corps.
They speak of glory, bravery,
Of victory and of pride,
But somewhere in the crowd,
A broken hearted mother cried.

They buried him in Arlington,
In a hallowed hero's grave,
Far from those for whom he'd
Traveled half a world to save.
And as the mournful music flows
From bugles, drums and pipes,
His mother's tears flow down
Upon the folded Stars and Stripes.

So, welcome all our heroes home
When this bloody war is won.
They've served their country admirably,
Their duty has been done.
But give a thought to those who've died,
And when the canons cease,
Let's all get on our knees and pray,
Please God, let there be peace.

75

FRIENDSHIP

Be seated, rest and set your burdens free,
Here, you're in the company of friends,
Gaze out at nature's calm serenity,
Breathe deep, the scented breezes that she sends.

Drink in the scene that stretches to the sky,
Let the brilliance of the sunset cleanse your soul,
Relax and let imagination fly,
Out above the vista you behold.

Soar with the gulls and eagles, wild and free,
Listen to the waves that lap the sand,
Let your troubles flow into the sea,
The scene you see is drawn by nature's hand.

Grief will pass and joy will re-appear,
For life's a circle; circles have no end.
So ease the mind and know that others care,
Refresh yourself and know you're welcome friend.

LITTLE HOUSE ASTRIDE THE STREAM

Memories will often cause a teardrop on my cheek,
(I'm really quite a sentimental guy.)
Like a small-unpainted outhouse, that stood astride the creek,
That I had to utilize in days gone by.
It was very sparsely furnished, just a bench seat with a hole.
The roof sometimes let in the rain and fog,
A door with leather hinges and a loosely packaged roll
Of paper from an Eaton's Catalogue.

In winter, I was full of dread, each time I had to go,
But I'd struggle through the snowdrifts to the door.
In knee-high boots and breeches, it was not a cinch, you know,
To complete this very necessary chore.
Snow blowing through the peephole turned to ice upon the floor.
In the frigid air, the seat was hard and cold.
Golden moonlight filtered through the cracks around the door,
And an icy gale blew upward through the hole.

But in summer, aah, in summer, in the balmy evening breeze,
With that battered door swung open to the air,
I could hear the breakers on the beach, and smell the salty sea,
And watch the little boats at anchor there.
I could sit alone and contemplate, contented and enthused,
About my future, and the things I hoped to do,
I could read the Eaton's catalogue, before it's put to use,
Life was simple then and troubles were so few.

Now I repose in warmth and comfort, on a softly padded seat,
'Mid painted walls and gleaming porcelain,
In winter I'm in heaven and appreciate this treat,
But in summertime my thoughts drift back again.

77

And I think about that open door, its perfect ocean views,
And I sometimes can't resist the urge to dream
Of those days I'd sit and contemplate, and read the shopping
news,
In that little shack that stood astride the stream.

GOLF IS A DANGEROUS GAME

Scotty waited on the tee, on a bench the pro had built,
With a bonnie lassie seated on his knee.
Rakish tam upon his head, a neatly fitted kilt,
A roguish and resplendent sight to see.
His foursome were astonished at the lassie on his lap,
For they had heard his reputation as a laddie.
They jokingly enquired if she was his handicap,
He answered "nae, she is ma ain wee caddy."

Then Scotty's features reddened and his confidence did wilt,
And a look of shock spread quickly o'er his face.
As he felt a sudden stirring from down deep beneath his kilt,
And he quickly moved his caddy from her place.
Then a tiny squirrel darted out from underneath his skirt,
Where it had climbed to partake of the heat.
Quivering, it hurried down his leg, into the dirt
And scurried in and out between his feet.

His caddie screamed in horror, his foursome laughed with glee.
The squirrel scurried off into the gorse.
Scotty smiled with some relief as he stood upon the tee,
Quite anxious to be out upon the course.
He was relieved it was a squirrel that created all the fuss,
That he'd suffered no embarrassment at all.
His caddie, searching in his bag and smiling back at us,
Said, "tis a'right Jock, it di'nae get your balls."

A BOOK OF CHILDHOOD MEMORIES

I found a tome within my mind,
Hid upon a secret shelf.
Nobody knows the secrets
Locked within it, but myself.
I stashed it many years ago
When I was just a boy,
Today when I reopened it
The contents brought great joy.

There was the ancient piece of slate
That I had used in school,
A compass and protractor,
Times tables, and a rule.
A blackboard and a leather strap
Were other things I saw,
As well as penny savings stamps,
To help us win the war.

Icicles hanging from the eaves
Down to the windowsill,
A steaming mug of cocoa malt
To ease the winter's chill.
Rabbit snares to be set out,
Firewood to bring,
Baby lambs and baby goats,
Appearing in the spring.

A gaily-painted spinning top,
A fishing line and hook,
A small toy boat, I used to sail
Up at aunt Bella's Brook.
A bamboo pole with shopping string,
A bobber painted red,
A mug-up by the crystal pond,
Cold tea and lassy bread.

Blue berries hanging from the bush,
The smell of new- mown hay.
Small sails coming into view,

Far out across the bay.
Codfish spread out on the flakes,
In the summer sun to dry,
Pitching buttons on the road,
Handmade kites to fly.

Skating on the frozen marsh,
Swimming at the beach.
Sliding down the snow clad hills,
A taste of homemade screech.
Memories are popping up
Everywhere I look.
Time to face reality.
I guess I'll close the book.

THE JOURNEY

As I begin my journey,
Where each must go alone,
I ask no grief or darkened rooms,
No sad and mournful tone.
Just celebrate the life I've had,
With friends all gathered near,
Smile at all the good times past,
But never shed a tear.

No tales of sadness do I want,
No words of doubt or fear.
For though in body I'll have gone,
In spirit, I am here.
I've lived a good and fruitful life,
Blessed by heaven above,
Been fortunate in friends I've had,
Been loved and given love.

And though you cannot feel my touch,
Nor earthly body see,
I will be there to comfort you
Each time you think of me.
And surely, as the darkest night,
Retreats before the dawn,
You'll come to know that even though
I've left; I am not gone.

THE BARFLY

He teeters on his bar stool in a cold flea bitten dive,
Bleary eyed and suffering the "shakes".
He barely eats enough these days, to keep himself alive,
But he'll get his drinks by any means it takes.
He's been out on the corner and he's bummed himself a buck,
He has hustled anybody who came near.
Now he's cold and wet and hungry but he knows, with any luck.
The bartender will let him have a beer.

He's a lost soul and a failure, but it wasn't always thus,
He was once a man, successful in his trade.
He had a home and family, much like any one of us,
Then he blew it in a game of "Ace-Away".
It was just one night of pleasure, just a friendly little game,
With newfound friends he'd met the day before.
They treated him to whiskey till he didn't know his name,
Then they led him to the dice game on the floor.

They stripped him of his bank account, and praised him as he lost,
They stripped him of his furniture and home.
He sat and rolled the loaded dice, unmindful of the cost,
Unmindful of the bitter days to come.
They slapped him proudly on the back, laughing at his jokes,
They urged him on to roll one final time.
Then when it was over, when assured that he was broke,
They left him in the street without a dime.

When he woke up in the gutter, not a penny to his name,
Disgusted with the thing that he'd become.
Filled with self-pity and remorse, he hung his head in shame,
And he turned to his remaining friend, the rum.
So he fell into the bottle, and he never could recover,
Folks jeer at him and treat him like a fool,
Then drop a quarter in his hat just to tide him over,
But they laugh to see him teeter on his stool.

I'LL BE THERE

You won't see me standing beside you,
While you're watching the change of the tide,
But never forget for a moment,
That I'll always be there at your side.

I'll be there in the glow of the sunset,
I'll be there in the blue of the sea,
Each spring when you hear that first robin,
You will know it's a message from me.

I'll be there on the course when you're golfing,
I will be at the rink for your game.
Whatever it is you are doing,
I'll be cheering you on just the same.

I'll be there in the bloom of the roses,
I'll be there when the spring blossoms start,
For although you may no longer see me,
I will always be close to your heart.

So at times when the loneliness hovers,
When the load seems too heavy to bear,
Just cherish our great years together,
And always believe I am there.

PLAY BALL

I love to watch a baseball game.
It's ever so relaxing.
It's slow enough to follow play
And never over-taxing.
But of late, the game that now is played
On artificial grass,
Is not the gentle game it was,
It's vulgar, bold and crass.

Starting with the nation's anthem
Which once was sung with pride,
It's now sung by a rapper
With a guitar at his side.
The teams line up on base paths
And as the country watches,
Right hands are placed above the heart,
Left hands are scratching crotches.

"Play Ball", the umpire hollers
And the batter's at the plate,
He fidgets with equipment while
The opposition waits.
He readjusts his helmet
Then three times he taps the plate,
Then steps back from the batters box,
As the pitcher glares with hate.

He glances to the dugout
Where the subs and coaches sit.
The dugout floor is littered
With tobacco juice and spit.
The announcer's spouting drivel,
As the starting pitch is near,
But half the fans have left their seats
To get another beer.

The batter swings, a double
Goes careening off the bat.
The second baseman greets him

With a friendly smile and pat.
It's not like watching Williams,
Mantle or DiMaggio.
Oh, where did all the rivalry
And competition go.

The baseball game that once I watched
And marveled at the skills,
Provided loads of entertainment,
Energy and thrills.
If they'd just get back to basics,
It would be a joy to me,
To see a game of baseball played
As it was meant to be.

VOICES FROM THE PAST

When I return to the Yukon,
Which I'm sometimes prone to do.
It's not because I feel the urge to roam.
It's because of little voices
That are calling out to me,
Calling, softly calling, "Come back home."

They are voices from my early days,
When I was but a youth,
In scarlet coat, sworn to uphold the right,
Voices of the midnight sun,
Soft voices from the Dome,
And the voices of the darkest winter nights.

There are voices from the vastness
Of the Yukon wilderness,
Of mountains that are wild and yet un-named.
Voices from the placid lakes,
Where the fighting fishes wait,
And the voice of endless rivers still untamed.

There's a voice that tells the solitude
Of the lonely hunting trail.
The voice of old prospectors seeking gold.
And the voices of the trapper,
Deep inside his cabin walls,
Contented and protected from the cold.

I'll obey those nagging voices
And again I'll journey back,
To see the northern lights, and be at peace,
And renew some ageing friendships,
That withstand the passing years,
For this is the land where friendships never cease.

THE IRON MAN OF THE NORTH

He walked the trail of ninety-eight,
To join the rush for gold.
Out from Cape Breton's rugged shore,
To the Yukon's frigid cold.
When he got to Dawson City,
He found that all the ground was staked,
He'd have to try another trade,
If his fortune he would make.

Then Percy won a contract
To deliver the Royal Mail,
Two hundred miles of heartache,
On the Dawson to Eagle trail.
Two hundred miles of river ice,
And drifting arctic snow,
Through mountains, swamp and tundra,
Where no road would ever go.

He brought the mail by freight canoe,
Horseback or dogs and sleigh,
Through spring floods or winter blizzards,
He would always find a way.
If mere mortals couldn't make it,
It's a cinch that Percy can,
That's why throughout the Yukon,
He was called the Iron Man.

Now each year they run a dog team race
Along that famous trail,
In honour of this mighty man
Who always brought the mail.
Forty years against the elements,
He and his dog teams fought,
To be renowned for ever
As the Iron Man of the north.

A SENIOR MOMENT

I woke up in the darkness
In the middle of the night,
With a title for a poem
In my head.
I contemplated getting up
And turning on a light,
But decided to compose it
In my bed.

So in the inky blackness,
I would formulate a line,
Then commit it to my memory
For the time.
Then I'd search my inner word-bank,
Until finally I would find
A corresponding phrase that
Seemed to rhyme.

In this way I wrote a poem
That would put my name in lights.
It was romantic and was
Masterfully done.
If there ever was a masterpiece
Composed in bed at night,
I am thoroughly convinced this
Is the one.

When done, I slept the night away.
Dreaming of success.
I was a poet much contented
With my lot.
When I awakened in the morning
I went rushing to my desk,
To put it down on paper,
But I'd forgot.

THE CAMERA OF JAMIE MACDUFF

Now Jamie MacDuff, he was Scottish enough,
With the blood of a Highland Clan.
And wherever he'd tarry, forever he'd carry
His digital camera in hand.
When for parties they gather, most people would rather
Dispense with the pictures and stuff,
They may think they are hid, but they cannot get rid,
Of the Camera of Jamie MacDuff.

When his grandchildren reach for a shell on the beach,
Or go for a swim in the ocean,
It will be there to catch every movement of each,
And to note every action or motion.
When they ride on the board it is there to record,
Every trick, be it easy or tough,
They may wake-board all day, but they can't get away
From the Camera of Jamie MacDuff.

When his friends come around for a night on the town,
Or the family and in-laws drop by,
They may sit there and gape, but they cannot escape,
The range of that hideous eye.
They may hide under cover, but still it will hover,
And they know they'll be caught soon enough,
Whether formally posed or just picking their nose,
By the Camera of Jamie MacDuff.

So if you have a reason, on a future occasion
To visit with Jamie some day,
Remember that you will be there in full view
Of that camera that's hidden away.
And if you've the right to remain overnight.
If you're prone to repose in the buff,
You'll be caught in the end by that wandering lens
Of the Camera of Jamie MacDuff.

THE CHRISTMAS GOOSE
(A Yukon Love Story)

Klondike Jack lived in a shack in the suburb of Whiskey Flats
Where Northern lights shone brightly through the gloom.
And his thoughts they strayed to a dusky maid, a princess of her
tribe,
With whom he'd love to share his board and room.
But she was wise to the ways of guys, and Christmas time was near,
So she'd offer her favors the day he could produce,
And bring to her, for holiday fare, a treat for which she yearned,
A fat and tender succulent Christmas goose.

So Jack he swore that he'd rest no more, 'til he'd return to her,
With a goose whose meat was tender and so fat,
That the dusky maid with raven braids would leave her tribal
home,
And share his bed and board on Whiskey Flats.
High and low through the ice and snow, he hunted day by day,
The woods were rife with ptarmigan and moose.
But never a sign could he ever find in that stark and frozen land,
Of the thing he wanted most, a Christmas goose.

The days they passed until at last, he spotted on the trail,
A raven perched atop a winter kill.
Though the man was near, it showed no fear; it gnawed its frozen
fare,
It stood its ground and greedily ate its fill.
It was big of bone and it weighed a stone, its feathers black as
night,
Its raucous voice spewed out its bold abuse.
"It's late" thought Jack, "I must get back, the Festive Season's
near,
I guess I'll improvise my Christmas Goose."

He quickly aimed, the rifle flamed, and the raven squawked and
fell,
He cleaned and plucked it featherless and bare,
The skin was rough, the drumsticks tough, the breast meat thick
and hard,
So unappetizing Jack could only stare.
And as he stared he greatly feared, the challenge he would have,
To turn this gristly hulk into a treat,

Then as he strained his fertile brain a sudden thought occurred,
"Of course" he cried, "I'll tenderize the meat."

When Jack got back to Whiskey Flat, determined to succeed,
In capturing his maiden, so aloof.
He headed for the liquor store, with the raven in his hand,
And bought a crock of Yukon overproof.
He grabbed the bird without a word, and he spread the opening some,
He thought of the maid and her promise of Christmas Day.
He shoved a hose 'neath the Papal Nose, and trickled in the rum,
Then with a smile he hid the corpse away.

Christmas Day dawned cold and gray, at noon the maiden came,
Her jet-black hair, in braids hung down her back.
She marveled at the table set with the finest paper plates,
And the plastic decorations 'round the shack.
When Klondike Jack retrieved the rack from out the oven hot,
With wholesome smells, the maid was overcome.
The pleasant scent of peppermint, of cloves and garlic salt,
And over all the faintest hint of rum.

When the treat of roasted meat was served up on her plate,
The flesh was browned and excellently done.
Then until late, they ate and ate the tasty, tender meat,
'Till nothing was remaining but the bone.
And when at last the evening passed he shyly walked her home,
They kissed, and she was loath to turn him loose,
With giddy head she turned for bed, to sleep, perhaps to dream
Of her lover and his gift, a Christmas Goose.

Now Klondike Jack has sold his shack and gone from Whiskey Flats,
No longer does he walk those hunting trails,
He and the maid with raven braids with their children, half a score,
Reside in luxury in Riverdale.
And though as yet he won't admit the cooking of that raven,
His wife will smile and offer no excuse.
Well-knowing she went willingly into his little haven,
And happily received her Christmas goose.

OLD FRIENDS

Acquaintances are commonplace,
You make them every day.
They come into your life and then
As quickly fade away.
But old friends, some you haven't seen
For months or even years.
Are staunch and if they're needed,
They always will be near.

Old friends are those who've hung in there,
Down through the passing years.
They've laughed with you in good times,
And in bad times, dried your tears.
They've celebrated nuptials,
And rejoiced at times of birth,
Been there for you when loved ones,
Were returned to Mother Earth.

Old friends you seldom think about
When things are going right,
It's not until that moment in
The middle of the night,
When all your dreams have crumbled,
And it seems your world will end
When you remember that you have,
An old and faithful friend.

So you, old friend, remember this,
As we cruise this rocky road,
I'll always be around for you,
To help you share the load.
I hope you feel that I have been,
Through good and troubled times,
As much a presence in your life,
As you have been in mine.

THE BALLAD OF SOAPY SMITH

When Soapy Smith the con man came to Skagway for the rush,
It was on to Dawson City he was bound.
To fleece successful miners toiling out there in the bush,
And relieve them of the nuggets that they found.

But while on the trail to Dawson to be closer to the gold,
In what he thought would be a lawless land,
He would meet Sam Steele, the Mountie and with certainty was
told
There would be no room for Soapy and his band.

Sam Steele told Soapy then and there, and in no uncertain terms,
That if the innocent he meant to fleece,
He had best get back to Skagway, or he very soon would learn
The justice of our Royal Mounted Police.

Soapy then returned to Skagway, where he built a gaming hall,
With its tables and its sporting girls so bold,
Who would lure the lonely miners heading southward in the fall,
To his lair where crooked dealers stole their gold.

He bought the politicians, set his henchmen on the bench,
As he set himself above the rule of law.
Businessmen were terrorized, and even governments
Closed their eyes to evidence they saw.

He ran the town of Skagway with a heavy iron fist,
With his ragged mob he murdered and he stole.
Prospectors and pioneers, with no power to resist,
Were assaulted 'til they offered up their gold.

He carried on his thievery so blatantly and bold,
He was a brazen bully and a knave.
Any action of resistance, an attempt to break his hold

Resulted in a cold and lonely grave.

Soapy was an evil man without one saving grace,
With a reputation now of some renown.
He looked with scorn on everyone, 'til the day he had to face
Frank Reid, the young surveyor of the town.

Frank vowed on his honor that he would bring Soapy down,
Folks jeered him and branded him a fool
He loaded up his pistol and he sent the word around,
That he would challenge Soapy to a duel.

Soapy Smith received the challenge at his table, playing cards,
And he saw his hands were shaking in the gloom,
He felt a strange sensation as he organized his guards,
An eerie premonition of his doom.

One July night in ninety-eight they met upon the dock
Two pistols blazed as one, and two men fell.
Frank Reid was sorely wounded and lay dying from the shock,
But he smiled when told that Soapy went to Hell.

Soapy died a desperado, a murderer and thief,
There were few who came to mourn his loss.
Frank Reid was hailed a hero for the way he came to grief,
Yet each now rests in Skagway 'neath a cross.

THE CHALLENGE OF MILES CANYON

While standing on the canyon wall,
A place I come to contemplate,
I seem to hear stampeders call
Down the trail of ninety-eight.
I see the boats of native wood
Built by men with skill and zeal,
Each loaded with a ton of goods,
Wooden boats, but men of steel.

I watch the small flotilla race
Down the waters of lake Marsh,
And then in single file they face
The challenge of the river harsh.
It's spring, the Yukon's in full flood,
The icy current strong and swift,
Yet nothing stems the festive mood
Until they enter 'tween the cliffs.

Into that yawning canyon mouth
The raging river roils and churns.
I hear a scream of fear ring out
As boats soar high and overturn.
They crumble on the rocky face,
While others go careening by.
Nothing stops this frantic race,
Some will live, but some must die.

The narrow canyon falls behind,
They rush into the river wide.
Around a rocky bend they wind,
And plunge into a raging tide.
The Whitehorse Rapids wild and dark,
Tossing boats, like toys, on high.
Some survive to make their mark
In Dawson town, while others die.

While I watch, the boats emerge
From the rapids strangling grasp,
As down the long, long trail they surge,

96

On to Dawson – home at last.
A grizzled old stampeder spoke,
Calling me to follow him,
But at that moment I awoke,
From my daydream on the canyon rim.

THE BEGGAR

He stands beside the open door,
Upturned hat between his feet,
Just outside the liquor store,
Begging for enough to eat.

Worn out shoes and clothes in tatters,
Shaggy puppy at his side.
I wonder if to one he matters,
Unshaven, rough and glassy-eyed.

Amidst the lights and Christmas glow,
He looks so sad and out of place.
And yet, I thought, it seems to show
Divergence of the human race.

I tossed the change my purchase brought me,
He smiled and thanked me with a nod,
I recall a phrase my daddy taught me,
"There's me, but for the grace of God".

Then as I walk away I ponder,
This diverse world in which we live,
Where man can split a land asunder,
Yet find it in his heart to give.

CHILDISH BEHAVIOUR

I heard a man complaining loud,
Though not to me directly,
That children, when they form a crowd,
Will not behave correctly.
I wondered why he'd act so wild
About the antics of a child.

When we were young we did not drink,
Though I am loath to lord it.
Not that we wouldn't have, I think,
We just could not afford it.
But there were other things we did
Which must remain forever hid.

There was little teen-age violence then,
And well our parents knew it.
Where would children learn to hate,
When adults didn't do it.
The apple, so it seems to me
Will not fall distant from the tree.

When judging children, as we do,
One fault if we have any,
We concentrate upon the few
And thus ignore the many.
For every apple turned to rot,
There's hundreds that as yet have not.

So lets divert our energy,
Lets now refrain from preaching.
I think that things will work if we
Just concentrate on teaching.
Then maybe kids will follow too,
Not as we say, but as we do.

BIRDWATCHING

The seagull's not a bird of note,
Not beautiful like some.
It begs its meals from fishing boats,
It's really just a bum.
Then when the fishing boats have gone,
It dumps its garbage on my lawn.

The gander is such a faithful bird,
They say he mates for life.
But samples all the chicks, I've heard,
Before he picks a wife,
Monogamous but always looking,
Even while his goose is cooking.

The crow, now there's a bird, depressing,
Clad in its suit of ebony,
It hasn't any taste in dressing,
No drabber bird could ever be.
But man could learn a lot you know,
From that oh so cunning crow.

I wonder at the mallard drake,
So handsome, with his head of green.
When nature calls he'll always take,
The plainest mate I've ever seen.
I know the secret that he keeps,
Beauty's only feather-deep.

The coot's the clown of all the birds,
Entertaining all who see.
Its flying style is so absurd,
It never knows where it should be.
Devoid of any understanding,
It crashes every time on landing.

My favorite of all's the eagle,
Standing guard high in the tree.
Like a king, so strong and regal,
Sheltering his family.
The eagle, so it seems to me,

100

Would be an awesome enemy.

And so I sit and watch the birds,
Resplendent in their winter plumage.
Wishing I could have the words,
The words to pay them proper homage.
Would that poems I could pen,
As beautiful as feathered friends.

OUR SYD

Soon you will be turning ten.
Our youngest grandchild of the five,
It seems like only recently,
We waited for you to arrive.
Then when you did, what joy you brought,
To all of us awaiting you,
Mom and dad, your nana, papa,
Grandma and your grandpa too.

We've watched you through your baby years,
Moving forward stage by stage,
Like a song bird gaining freedom,
Bursting from its gilded cage.
We heard the first words that you uttered,
Watched you take each faltering step.
Shared your pride in every victory,
Anguished with you when you slipped.

We've been there to urge you onward,
Watched your triumphs through the years,
Shared your laughter when you're happy,
When you stumbled, dried your tears.
Now as you move to new beginnings,
Not a babe nor yet a teen,
But a child whose place in life,
Seems always somewhere in between.

You will find new worlds to conquer,
In the future, yet unknown.
But in your journey to discover,
You will never be alone,
You will have our love to guide you,
And you'll always know that we,
Will be there to walk beside you
As you seek maturity.

DEATH WATCH

He stood there in his prison garb,
Before the judges throne.
Just a boy of nineteen years,
So scared and all alone.
I saw his body stiffen
And tremble as from cold,
As the judge decreed, "may God
Have mercy on your soul."

He'd gotten in an argument,
And by too much booze, inspired,
When things were getting out of hand
He drew a gun and fired.
The judge and jury now have found
He freely chose to kill,
And so must face the penalty,
The gallows on the hill.

I led him to his prison cell
Where he would now repose,
And I would be his guard until
That final sun arose.
For days we talked, as young men do,
Of girls and dates and cars,
And played an endless game of cribbage
Through the prison bars.

He never spoke about his deed,
No comment of regret.
Showed no sorrow for his victim,
Or the way he'd met his death.
He kept his feelings hidden
In a soul so dark and deep,
But late at night I'd often hear him
Sobbing in his sleep.

Throughout the passing days I watched
For some sign of remorse.
For some sign of regret for taking

Such a destructive course.
But he maintained his silence,
Unrepentant 'till the day
I watched a grim old padre come
And lead the boy away.

ODORIFEROUS ODIE MacWHINE

In a forest up north in the Yukon,
In a cabin constructed of pine,
Lived a trapper, alone and neglected,
Odoriferous Odie MacWhine.
The name was bestowed by his mother,
As she suckled the babe in her bunk,
And she noticed a strange emanation,
An overpowering odor of skunk.

As Odie grew up into manhood,
All alone with the fauna and flora,
The young ladies would always ignore him,
Because of that distastful aura.
Yet he fell for a girl of the Tlinget,
A beautiful maiden named Nell,
She was also enamoured with Odie,
But she couldn't put up with the smell.

Then Odie, alone in his cabin,
Soaked his body with lotions and scents,
And he dressed in the finest of deerskin,
Then off to her tepee he went.
They entwined in a wild rage of passion,
As the maiden discarded her skirt,
But she fainted and fell, overcome by the smell,
When Odoriferous took off his shirt.

But Nell was a girl of conviction,
And at last when she rose from her bunk,
She went out to Odoriferous' trap line,
Where she captured a venomous skunk.
She returned to her tribe in the darkness,
And there in her tepee she stayed.
Where she sat on a trunk and petted that skunk,
Till it lifted its brush and it sprayed.

Poor Odie, so sad and dejected,
Remained in his cabin alone.
Until Nell came around and connected,

And he took her to wed as his own.
Now they're both living back in the forest,
In that cabin constructed of pine,
Folks call them Odoriferous Odie,
And Noxious Nellie MacWhine.

SINBAD

Sinbad is quite a handsome cat,
Jet black, with eyes that glow.
He has a better life style
Than many folks I know.
He's the king of all his realm,
He looks with scorn at me.
He's the master at the helm,
Like a captain while at sea.

He prowls throughout his castle,
Right of passage through the house,
Senses sharp, prepared to wrestle
Any brave intruding mouse.
Bold guardian of his station
He's the boss man, he's the head.
He demands no compensation
All he asks is to be fed.

He doesn't have to work each day,
Just hunts when in the mood.
He doesn't need to eat his prey,
He dines on gourmet food.
Some would say he's but a loafer,
But he'll insist he's just retired.
His place is on the sofa,
To be coddled and admired.

He's gained my admiration,
Oh, to be so cool and suave.
I'd be a man above my station,
If his karma I could have.
The lady cats all think that he
Would make a perfect suitor.
But that would not work out you see,
Alas, poor lad, his gender's neuter.

CAPTIVE OF THE NORTH

If you have stood upon the Dome
To watch the Midnight Sun,
Seen the beauty of the springtime bursting forth.
If you've seen the caribou roam,
Seen dog-team races run,
You'll forever be a captive of the north.

If you've seen the town of Dawson,
In the pale blue winter light.
Seen the Aurora Borealis all aglow.
If you've experienced the awesome
Yukon River, felt its might,
You're a northerner, no matter where you go.

If you've rode it's winding narrow rails,
Climbed its mountains, tall and stark,
Panned its nuggets from the crystal streams.
Walked the ancient gold rush trails,
Struggled through the winter's dark,
You will always see the Yukon in your dreams.

If you've seen the autumn freeze-up,
Stayed for break- up in the spring,
If you've trod the path along the canyon wall.
If you've ever made a camp-stop
Out beyond the arctic ring,
Then, my friend, you'll always hear the Yukon call.

If you've ever rode the river boats,
Through Five Fingers, unforgiving,
Seen the rapids where the water roils and froths.
If you've trailed the sheep and mountain goats
Then, no matter where you're living,
Your heart is set forever in the north.

SURVIVAL

Two mallards settled in the pond,
Upon the golf course where I play.
And over time, they built a nest
From bits of down and new-mown hay.
For days I watched as eagerly
They toiled to make their home secure,
Where they could raise their family,
Deep in the reeds along the shore.

I did not see them for a while,
At least not two of them together.
But he was always standing watch,
Upon the pond, despite the weather.
Then one day, she reappeared,
A mother now, and proud was she.
Behind her closely following,
Twelve tiny ducks, her family.

I thought of all the predators,
And for the little ones I feared.
I watched each day while passing by,
As, one by one, they disappeared.
How sad, I thought, in such a place
Where many creatures live and thrive,
Such tiny beings have to face,
The awesome struggle to survive.

The weeks went by and as they grew.
Attrition rate was so appalling,
That in the end a precious two
Survived to fly to natures calling.
And when they flew to warmer climes,
They left me feeling somewhat sad,
Why do I let things get me down,
When such an easy life I've had.

THE BAYMAN

He grew up beside the ocean,
Spent his childhood on the beach,
And learned his trade from elders in his clan.
He's been fishing since his early teens
Now he's about to teach
His grandson how to be a fisherman.

He has always been a slogger,
His hands are gnarled by toil,
His days are long with little time for rest.
He couldn't be a logger.
Or a tiller of the soil,
But put him in a boat and he's the best.

He dresses in his oilskins,
Not for him, the life romantic.
He would stifle in a pinstripe suit and tie.
With his oars set in the tholepins
He will brave the wild Atlantic,
But put him in an office and he'd die.

On Sunday at the altar
He's at peace before his God,
His boat is on the collar in the bay.
His cellar's full of vegetables,
His store is full of cod.
He's dependant on no other for his pay.

Cod fishing is his birthright,
He was born unto the sea.
He's a bayman, as his father was before.
May he always have the foresight
To ensure that there will be,
Conservation of the stock for evermore.

ELECTION DAY

For six weeks we're subjected to
A flood of politicians,.
Doling out goodies as they do,
Though subject to conditions.
"All health and welfare will be free,
But only if you vote for me."

Day after day I watch the news
And get the same old story –
Every person has his views,
Some are Liberal, some Tory.
The NDP is seldom seen,
And even less, the party Green.

They tell me, if I vote for Paul,
The Doctors won't be leavin',
And I won't have a care at all
If I cast my vote for Stephen.
But only if I vote for Jack
Will I get all my taxes back.

The whigs will wave the olive branch,
While Tories wave the sabre.
Quebec would tie its hopes to France,
Ontario to Labour,
While in B.C. we fear they're gonna'
Cast their vote for Marijuana

Party hacks will hire bands,
Praise their leaders to the skies.
Candidates will shake our hand,
Kiss our babies, tell us lies.
When it comes to righting wrongs,
They will speak with many tongues.

Would that I could find a way
To recognize an honest man,
When, upon Election Day,
I drop my ballot in the can.

Why to I feel that, to my sorrow,
Nothing will have changed tomorrow.

ON LOOKING AHEAD

When in our twenties life was sweet,
The road ahead of us was long.
No grass grew beneath our feet,
We lived for parties, wine and song.
"Life is for the young", we said,
And never paused to look ahead.

As our thirties came and went,
They were awfully busy years.
Day after day, our time was spent,
Juggling family and careers.
"These are busy times", we said,
And never paused to look ahead.

In our forties we're in our prime,
Blessed with health and energy,
Teenagers now consumed our time,
Little time for you and me.
"We still have lots of years," we said,
We never paused to look ahead.

Our fifties came, the kids have gone,
We've all the free time we require.
We're satisfied with what we've done
And plan our life when we retire.
"Our lives will now slow down," we said,
But never paused to look ahead.

Our sixties were a time of stress,
Interspersed with times of fun.
Some darker days, but none the less,
We had our winters in the sun.
"Life is sometimes harsh," we said,
Treasure each day, don't look ahead.

Now we're in our seventies,
And time for us is winding down,
As we look back in reverie,

Delighted that we're still around.
"One day at a time," we say
Tomorrow's just another day.

Take each day as it arrives,
Work to make each day worthwhile.
Keep perspective, in your lives
Always try to wear a smile.
"You never can go back" it's said,
Nor can you change what lies ahead.

LUNA

Luna was a killer whale, which was straying from its pod,
The natives seem to think 'twas Heaven-sent,
Its fate, as with all living things, was in the hands of God,
But that's not good enough for Government.
It would have to be protected from people and, in turn
The people must be sheltered from the whale.
The whale was courting fishing boats and very slow to learn
Its place in life, and thereby hangs the tale.

Luna just appeared one day, from out the foggy mists
And it soon became a hero of some note
It was over-fed and coddled by environmentalists
But a danger to the local fishing boats.
Then government decided that the whale would have to move
They'd capture it and take it to its clan.
The native band objected, claiming they could prove,
Luna was the reincarnate of a man.

We sent a mighty naval ship, with a massive wire cage,
To capture it and steal it like a thief.
The natives in their war canoes, approached them in a rage,
Claiming Luna as the spirit of their chief.
The government was adamant, poor Luna had to go,
Tax dollars came outpouring to the cause.
The natives with their war drums, stood up and shouted "no",
So the government declared another pause.

We sat at televisions and we daily watched the news,
All wondering which side would get its wish.
Was Luna from the spirit world, as in the native view?
Or was he just another giant fish?
Then while the battle raged and surged, 'twas Luna came to grief,
Whether killer whale, or true reincarnation,
He slipped away from everyone, swam out beyond the reef,
Now he's blubber at a Russian whaling station.

ODE TO ROBERT SERVICE

When he came from bonnie Scotland, the gold trail was inviting,
He was somewhat without aim, it seems to me,
'Til he joined the bank in Whitehorse, where he began his writing
Then he knew the Yukon was his destiny.

He was smitten by the vastness of the land to which he came,
And he wrote about the wonders he could see.
It was there he wrote the poems that would bring him instant fame,
The tales of Dan McGrew and Sam McGee.

He moved to Dawson City, and the moment he arrived,
He would find the isolation that he sought.
In his little moss chinked cabin his imagination thrived
And he wrote his tales and poems of the north.

He told stories of stampeders in the Klondike rush for gold,
And he told about the hardships and the cost.
Of toiling in the frozen muck, the hunger and the cold
And the fortunes easily made and quickly lost.

He told us of the women who had dared the goldrush trail,
Who fought the elements with all their might.
Wrote of brawny Mounties and the men who brought the mail,
And told of con men and ladies of the night.

He wrote about the solitude, the arctic winter nights,
Of flowers blooming 'neath the midnight sun.
Of law abiding Dawson, where Mounties kept the right,
And of Skagway with it's only law, the gun.

When called, he went to Europe, to the canon and the lance,
And his poems spoke of battles that were fought.
Then when the war was over he would settle down in France,
And never more see his beloved north

His name became a household word; he died a man of fame,
Each verse another feather in his cap,
Northerners forever more, will glorify his name,
Robert Service put the Yukon on the map.

HALLOWEEN

I sit and watch the evening news,
With all its troubles, blood and gore.
I pale at the announcers' views,
Then comes a knock upon my door.
A long and piercing scream I hear,
And after that, a troubled moan.
I try to overcome my fear,
But still my apprehension's growin'.

With trembling hands I turn the lock,
(I am a senior, gray and hobblin')
Out on my porch, much to my shock,
I spy a mob of ghosts and goblins.
One is just a skeleton,
His bones reflect an eerie glow.
One has a lighted halo on,
But he is not a saint, I know.

There's buccaneers in pirate masks,
Who boldly fly the Jolly Roger.
They've swords and guns and whisky flasks,
Enough to cow this spineless codger.
I see an ancient warty hag,
Draped in costume, long and loose.
A headless man, two dressed in drag,
And there's a hangman with his noose.

No good will come of this I know,
They've come to cause us hurt and pain,
They carry pillow sacks to stow
Their booty, ill begotten gains.
But it's my castle; I'm the king,
"What is it that you want", I bleat.
As one, their childish voices ring,
With joy and laughter "Trick or Treat."

As I top up their goody bags,
I have some feeling of chagrin,
Then shuffle back into my chair,

To watch the daily news again.
So thankful that I'm living free,
Where naught but this will cause me fright,
For its All Hallowed 'een, you see,
Ghosts and goblins roam tonight.

A THANKSGIVING PRAYER

Dear Lord, before we start this feast
Of turkey, vegetables and dressing,
Just for a moment let us pause
To thank you for our many blessings.
We thank you for the little gifts
That we have gained along the way.
We thank you for the lives we lead,
And thank you for this autumn day.

We thank you for our native land,
Where we may live and grow in peace,
And pray that we will see the day
When hate and prejudice will cease.
We thank you for the friends we have,
And now that we are old and sage,
We thank you for our memories,
And for our Yukon heritage.

We thank you for the warming sun,
As well for those April showers,
We thank you for all nature's gifts,
And for the right to call them ours.
We thank you for the fun we've shared,
And even for the tears we've cried.
Down through the years life has been good,
Please Lord let us be satisfied.

Now as we sit at this repast,
Of food and drink and all good stuff,
We hope some day 'twill come to pass,
That all God's children have enough.
And as we eat and share a quaff,
With loved ones whom we hold so dear,
We thank you, and with joy and hope,
Look forward to another year.

FOGGY MIDNIGHT

Roused from my restless slumber I arise,
As is my wont, I glance toward the strand.
No scene of peaceful grandeur do I spy,
No sound of rippling waves upon the sand.
The balcony is cold beneath my feet,
The air contains an icy autumn chill,
A muffled sound of traffic from the street,
Then the blare of sirens, loud and shrill.

As I peer into darkness so complete,
I cannot see where ocean touches sand.
An eerie stillness falls upon the street,
A heavy bank of fog enshrouds the land.
Somewhere at sea a foghorn rips the gloom,
The ghostly sound of tortured souls in flight.
I turn and hurry back into my room,
So grateful to be safe at home tonight.

THE TRUTH ABOUT JACK AND JILL

When Jack and Jill went up the hill,
They weren't just after water,
They were doing other things
They really hadn't ought'a.
Carrying the water pail
Was a most convenient cover,
For Jill was reaching puberty,
And Jack was quite a lover.

When they came tumbling down the bank,
The tale that they related,
I felt was nothing other than
A story they'd created.
While thinking thus, I told myself
I'd go and have a look
To see what they'd been doing,
While up there beside the brook.

Then at a spot beyond the well
Where farmers had been haying
I found a soft depression where
The couple had been laying.
I found some evidence around,
And after analyzing,
I didn't have the slightest doubt,
That they'd been fraternizing.

The couple had been smoking grass
(And I'm not talking hay)
The butts were scattered 'round about
In a most unsightly way.
The broken glass and bottle caps
Left me quite aghast,
It seemed to me that Jack and Jill
Had had themselves a blast.

So shed no tears for clumsy Jack,
He never broke his crown,
In fact he'd not have fallen

121

If he'd not been "fooling around",
And little Jill now owns the hill,
After finding she could sell
Most anything she wanted to,
Up there beyond the well.

TO THE VICTOR GOES THE SPOILS

While sunning at the beach one day, my mind a total blank,
Which some would say could be most any day.
I spied a crow in formal black, perched high upon a bank,
Intent upon the action in the bay.

Now many folks would class the crow a rascal and a sinner,
Not a subject upon which to waste one's time.
Yet I could see that, just like me, it's waiting for its dinner,
But, unlike me, it wouldn't cost a dime.

I watched the tide recede until an object caught my eye.
An oyster that the ocean left behind.
It would make a tasty morsel and it's stranded high and dry,
"Aha" says I, " there's dinner and its mine."

But in the time it took for me to rise from my position,
And waddle out to claim my lawful prize,
The crow, which proved to be in far superior condition,
Had grabbed the shell and soared into the skies.

While in a rage I cursed that bird and all its sorry clan,
And hurled my condemnation to the sky.
To demonstrate its attitude of bold contempt for man,
It dropped a juicy bomb as it flew by.

It dropped the oyster on a rock and broke the pearly shell,
Then it mocked me as it ate its stolen snack.
Though I could see disaster coming I just sat and laughed like hell,
When a mighty eagle landed on its back.

GETTING TOGETHER
(Christmas luncheon 2004)

Once again we meet from diverse places,
To share a laugh and raise the cup of cheer,
With joy we see the old familiar faces
Of people we have treasured through the years.

We'll talk of days long gone, but still remembered,
The midnight sun and happiness and flowers,
Days of our June, when now it's our December,
Days of our youth, when all the world was ours.

We'll talk of grown up kids and new grandchildren,
Of wedding bells and anniversaries,
We'll talk of friends, who count their wealth in millions,
And others who exist on memories.

We'll talk of long lost trails we've trod together,
In that majestic land which calls us yet.
A land of happy times and awesome weather,
That we have left behind yet can't forget.

The land that keeps its hold on those she's chosen,
Those who would be known as sourdoughs,
For though we've felt her wrath, and damn near frozen,
The yearning for the Yukon only grows.

While we've retreated now to warmer climes
Recalling all the battles that we fought
We never can forget those happy times,
When we were young and living in the north.

Yet as we hug with tears of joy and gladness,
That we are back for yet another year.
We'll also share a brief moment of sadness,
In memory of friends no longer here.

THE ROCKET RACER SLED

I still recall when I was small, on the shore at Bishops Cove,
At Christmas time I cut a pine out back in papa's grove.
I dragged it back to our humble shack for my mom and dad to
see,
They praised their son for a job well done, and they praised my
Christmas tree.

Well I couldn't wait to decorate and trim that little pine,
And standing there in the frosty air great happiness was mine.
Then that long long pause for Santa Claus to visit on Christmas Eve.
While I dreamed at night of the gifts I'd like and wondered what
he'd leave.

And I thought "not much, just socks and such", and I fought to
hold back tears,
To the folks full grown, those times were known as the great
depression years.
But I had looked in a shopping book, as I lay at night in bed,
It was hopeless yet my heart was set on a Rocket Racer sled.

I woke at dawn that Christmas morn and searched beneath the
tree,
But though I took a thorough look, there was little there for me.
I turned apart with heavy heart, from my meager little toys,
And went outside, my grief to hide, and play with other boys.

Then as I stooped to open up the back porch storage shed,
There on the floor inside the door was my rocket racer sled.
Red and sleek with bed of teak it surely was a stunner,
With painted stars and handlebars and shiny iron runners.

This year I'll watch my grandkids search a mountainous pile of gifts,
And I'll laugh for joy with each girl and boy, to see their spirits lift.
But they'll never see such outright glee as their old papa had,
With his first spill down a snow clad hill on his Rocket Racer sled.

SASQUATCH

I thought I saw a sasquatch running through the snow,
Leaping through the timber where a rabbit couldn't go.
It had a hairy body and a very funny shape,
Its father was a grizzly bear; its mother was an ape.
It rambled over mountain tops and down into the glen,
I swore that I would trap one, but I couldn't catch it then.
I couldn't climb the mountain as fast as it could go,
I thought I would out-smart him, deliberate and slow.

I trailed that ugly sasquatch for countless winter days,
From inside the arctic circle down to the Kootenays.
And when I finally found him, hiding in a cave,
I thought "you beast, I've got you," but I wasn't all that brave.
I decided just to sit around and try to wait him out.
My tent was stocked with alcohol and lots of food about.
That night I heard a whining, and a scratching at my door,
And there was Mr. Sasquatch with a beer mug in his paw.

He smiled at me real friendly like, I swear to God he did,
I offered him a bottle and he quickly snapped the lid.
And so we drank the night away and shared a moose stew pot,
The conversation wasn't much; he smiled and scratched a lot.
Then he crawled outside the tent where snow was soft and deep,
He crawled into a hollow and was quickly sound asleep.
I too slept the night away and when I woke at dawn,
I went to get my sasquatch but, the bugger he was gone.

I had to find my sasquatch and get him back again,
So I had a bite of breakfast and another flask of gin.
I found his trail and followed it up to a mountain peak,
Found him with a whiskey glass and frying up a steak.
He turned and smiled a welcome and pointed to a glass
I knew I'd had sufficient but I'm never one to pass.
In total relaxation he was propped against a stump,

126

But when I reached to shake his hand, he turned around and
jumped.

I hurried down the mountainside to the valley floor below,
There wasn't any sign of him, no footprints in the snow.
I've never found a trace of him nor seen another one,
But sometimes when I'm all alone I miss the hairy son.
Most people tend to doubt my tale (as if I'd tell a lie),
They think I'm just a little strange, I can't imagine why,
I know I saw a sasquatch, I know I saw him fall,
But did I see him in the flesh or in the alcohol.

MIRACLES

When God designed the universe
'Twas fraught with danger, gloom and ills,
Too dark and cold to nurture life,
So He performed some miracles.

For warmth He made the blazing sun,
Then moon and stars to light the earth,
And later He created life,
And thus, the miracle of birth.

For beauty He made flowers and trees,
Little fawns and angels wings,
Rainbows after every storm,
And a myriad of birds that sing.

The brilliance of the setting sun,
That tells us when each day is gone,
And then, when we have rested well,
To wake us up He brings the dawn.

He gave us little humming birds,
And mighty eagles soaring high,
The right to love, the will to laugh,
The wonder of a baby's cry.

He gave us gentle butterflies,
And the power of great waterfalls.
The serenity of lily ponds,
And awesome snowcapped mountains tall.

He filled the earth with living things,
In fields of green and crystal waters,
And then at last, He gave the world
His masterpiece, my three granddaughters.

TSUNAMI

Christmas time, a time of peace,
Vacationers from round the earth,
Gathered on that distant shore
To celebrate the Savior's birth,
Families from many lands,
Content and basking on the sand.

Then by some freak of nature's plan,
Not understood by you or me,
A giant tremor shook the earth,
From deep beneath the placid sea.
The sea, in anger, roils and raves,
Creating mighty tidal waves.

On shore the hordes of people stared,
In horror, fear and disbelief,
As giant waves came rushing forth
To sweep the land beyond the reef.
In fear they fled for higher ground,
A sanctuary never found.

For onward rolled the angry seas
As through the land it ripped and tore,
Destroying homes, uprooting trees,
And washing all away from shore.
While those who fled the tidal wave,
Were fleeing to a watery grave.

Entire towns were overcome,
And borne away into the deep,
Thousands swept to pain and death,
With few survivors left to weep.
Parents torn from little ones,
Torn from sisters, brothers, sons.

And then the sea was calm again,
Lapping at the burning sand,
While an eerie silence loomed,
O'er the ravaged empty land.

129

Survivors stood in agony,
Staring numbly out to sea.

Only time will heal the wounds,
Time will take the hurt away,
But people watching round the world,
Will nevermore forget that day.
The day the Master called the roll
And claimed three hundred thousand souls.

OUR FALLEN HEROES

I had a dream the other night,
While safe at home in bed.
I saw four young men passing,
In their brilliant coats of red.
They were riding jet-black horses,
And went streaming through the sky,
While far off in the distance
I could hear the people cry.

As the riders passed before me,
I was summoned from my bed,
And I watched as they saluted,
Then one turned to me and said,
"We have tried to do our duty,
We have stood the final test,
Now to you we pass the banner,
Hold it high and do your best."

"We have stood to serve our country,
Took the blows and bore the pain,
Now we offer you the challenge,
Let our deaths be not in vain.
Do not let the force of evil
Win the battle that we've fought,
Lest all who've gone before us
Were sacrificed for naught."

Then I wakened in the confines
Of my comfortable domain.
And I thought of four young Mounties,
Who so recently were slain,
I thank my God for men like those,
Who walk the streets alone,
That we may sleep in peace tonight,
In the safety of our home.

REFLECTIONS

He stared at me accusingly,
This tired, worn old man,
As if 'twas me, caused him to be
So bent and pale and wan.
As if 'twas I, caused time to fly
Ever more quickly now.
I wonder why, he thinks that I
Am responsible, somehow.

I didn't know that he would go
So quickly through this life.
Why should I feel responsible
For his troubles, grief or strife?
So with a frown, I stare him down,
I won't accept, I vow.
I'll bear no shame, nor take the blame
For the furrows in his brow.

He cannot say I caused the gray,
Where once thick dark hair grew.
Nor can he blame his lack of fame
On anything I do.
With nothing said, he turns his head,
As I too, turn away.
I turn and go, and yet I know,
We'll meet another day.

For that's the way it is each day,
It's really quite absurd,
He'll imitate each move I make
Yet utter not a word.
If I wave, he too will wave,
He'll meet but will not pass.
Just stare at me reproachfully,
From within that looking glass.

COLUMBIA

Giant spaceship streaking through the sky,
Fifteen minutes out from base, and home.
Seven astronauts, their duty done,
Thoughts of glad reunions soon to come.
Men and women confident and bold,
Destined to push back the last frontier.
They've been in space, where few on earth have been,
They've earned the admiration of their peers.

Back on earth, an anxious world awaits,
Tuned in to see the landing from the blue.
Then that dreaded headline on the screen,
"Breaking news. Columbia's overdue".
A hush creeps over all the world, it seems,
Seconds pass like hours as we wait.
Hoping against hope someone will say,
All is well, the ship is merely late.

Then, those chilling pictures on the screen,
Grey-white contrails through the Texas sky.
Smoking debris streaking to the ground,
As watchers weigh the cost and wonder "why".
Columbia is gone, her work is done,
Yet she will live in stories of her fame.
And seven souls go streaking through the sky,
Destined for the heavens, whence they came.

FINIS

I write of olden days, events long past,
Of people that I've met along my way.
Some who have touched my life, and just as fast,
Have vanished from the scene while others stay.
Of pioneers who toiled with pick and pan,
And helped to shape the Yukon at it's birth,
The hardy fishermen of Newfoundland,
Who brave the stormy seas and prove their worth.
I've written too, of things I do for leisure,
Of fishing, golf, and walking by the sea.
Of animals and birds that bring such pleasure,
And of old friends who mean so much to me
I've told of men who dared, and stood the test,
Who won or lost but, either way, they tried.
I've written too, of friends who've gone to rest,
Who fought the battle well before they died.
If you can say, " I knew those people too,"
If you can say " I too recall those times,"
If you can say "the tales he tells are true"
Then I can rest, contented with my rhymes.

POETRY AND OTHER NONSENSE

A collection of verse by

Gus Barrett.

Copies of this book may be obtained directly from
the Author at:-

7 – 2734 West Island Hwy
Qualicum Beach, B.C.
V9K1P7

Phone 1-250-752-0312
e-mail sourdoughs2@shaw.ca

Price $20.00 per copy, includes shipping costs.

ABOUT THE AUTHOR

Gus Barrett was born in Bishops Cove, Nfld. in 1930. In 1944 the family moved to St. Johns where Gus attended St. Michael's High School and one year of business school, then went to work at the post office. One year later, after Newfoundland entered into confederation with Canada, he joined the R.C.M.P. After a six month training course in Rockcliffe, Ont., he was transferred to Toronto and then to Sault Ste. Marie. In 1953 he was transferred to the Yukon where he served in Whitehorse and Dawson City. While in the Yukon he met and married Blanche Holbrook of Dawson City. Gus left the force at that time and worked for the next 12 years for various Government departments, including a stint with the Canadian Customs on the Alaskan Border. In 1967 he was working for the Canada Manpower Center and was transferred to Trail, B.C. While there he was promoted to manager and transferred to Quesnel, B.C. and then in 1973 to Port Alberni B.C. He retired in 1985.

Gus and Blanche are now located at Qualicum Beach where they spend their free time on the golf course. They have three children and five "exceptional" grand children.

Gus started writing poetry at the ripe old age of 69. The good memories of time spent in both Newfoundland and the Yukon are apparent in many of his poems.

ISBN 1-41206162-8